It's Complicated

To Juan
Happy Reading
Michele x

It's Complicated

...

Michele Paul

The Book Guild Ltd

First published in Great Britain in 2019 by
The Book Guild Ltd
9 Priory Business Park
Wistow Road, Kibworth
Leicestershire, LE8 0RX
Freephone: 0800 999 2982
www.bookguild.co.uk
Email: info@bookguild.co.uk
Twitter: @bookguild

Typeset in Adobe Garamond Pro

Printed and bound by CPI Group (UK) Ltd, Croydon, CR0 4YY

ISBN 978 1912881 802

British Library Cataloguing in Publication Data.
A catalogue record for this book is available from the British Library.

To Tara

CONTENTS

1
• • •

ONLINE DATING
HERE I COME!

So, you thought it was going to last forever.

You loved him. Made compromises. Allowed for his little irritating habits. You were committed and still, it wasn't enough. It was not the 'Happily Ever After' you thought it was going to be, but you made the best of it. You had chosen him and were trying your hardest to make the 'forever after' work.

He would have been quite happy to stay with you forever, as long as you continued the cooking, cleaning, sorting out the bills, holidays etc., and allowed him to continue seeing other people. When you finally realised that there was always going to be someone else in his life, possibly not prettier nor funnier than you. You had to accept the fact that he had a significant other and it was no longer you.

After the heartaches, the arguments, the tears, the denials, you eventually separate and you are left torturing yourself wondering what you did wrong, what you could have done differently, what had actually happened. Until one day a year or so later, the postman delivers a letter to your address. A hotel bill. With two names on the receipt: your ex and a lady. Surprisingly enough, not the one he cheated on you with and now living with. Another lady. This explained why I received the invoice from the hotel; he couldn't have given his real address!! It was safer giving his old address than the new one.

A lifelong relationship is a state of mind and one day, you come to the conclusion that there was nothing you could have done. You were the only one in the relationship with that state of mind, at least the monogamous part of it.

And yet here you are; the one alone and middle aged trying to embark in a new chapter of your life. Not such an easy task when your self-confidence is rock bottom!

First, you need to re-build the little self-esteem you had. When you do feel a little better, you realise that he wasn't at all what you thought he was. Definitely not 'The One' for the rest of your life. Not even close! You had been mistaken all along and your search for the 'Real One' had to begin.

Meanwhile, it's meals for one in front of the TV and no one to have a chat with from the minute you are back from work. On the other side of the coin, no one to argue with, no one to untidy the house! No one! At times being alone gets to you and it is an easy step to cross over before you start feeling lonely and incredibly miserable too.

Your friends, the ones still enjoying perfect relationships and family lives, will more often than not tell you that they envy the peace and quiet of your new life, only because they can still enjoy the happy, busy family banter most days. When you are stuck at home day after day in front of your ready meal it is not the same story and quite honestly the novelty of a quiet evening in soon wears off.

They will always offer advice and recommend you to join clubs and societies to get out and meet people. It is pointless reminding them that it is something you had already been doing for years. You may have been in a dead-end relationship, but you still had a life with hobbies and friends.

So, join more activities? Leave the ones you enjoyed and start new ones? Carry on with the ones you have been doing for years when you know there are none available for you?

And what do you do for the holidays?

I was fortunate enough to be able to go on holiday with family and friends most of the time, but there were times when I had no companions to share my annual leave with.

I also discovered the joys of solo holidays, where people in the same situation as you mix up for a week or so. I must confess that these holidays were not just a godsend but a massive laugh too.

Eventually, tagging along as a singleton with your coupled friends can become tedious and once you have regained some self-confidence and self-esteem and you think, "Well I still have much to offer and I am missing the complicity and intimacy of a relationship, so why can't I start a new chapter?" Different people connect at a different point in their lives, so why not now?

How do you go about meeting that new person when you have been with someone for so many years?

And with this begins the minefield of online dating, because despite all your friends saying, "You'll meet a nice man, there's someone for everyone," they never introduce you to anyone single and you decide to embark in the world of online dating.

It is that simple.

Or is it?

If you are single in today's world it is going to be very difficult for you to avoid the online dating adventure. Most of the single people I know are, or have been, dating online. Sometimes you hear a very happy story; people have met online, clicked, literally, got married and are living happily ever after as we speak. So why not me?

Some end up disappointed and cynical, but as a rule of thumb if you have been single at any point in your life you have been online and as such, you are bound to be on the same site as some people you know. And, of course, this happened to me.

You already know many people who have met their current partners via online dating sites and who are keen to recommend them. In a flash, you have access to thousands of potential partners and you can see, who you already share interests with, see a picture... easy. Swipe right for yes, left for no. How difficult can it be to find 'The One' ?

The internet is flooded with various sites; which one to choose from? There is even a compare the online dating site website to assist you. The comparative website will tell you how user-friendly the dating site is, how big the databases are, testimonies, prices, etc.

You may choose to go on a comparative website to select your dating site or make your selection based on personal recommendation or both. Although the personal recommendation is not always a good idea, as you will share the same database of potential partners with your friends.

Anyway, you make the first step and go 'online' . You have selected a site, you are almost good to go.

Registering is usually free and easy.

After that, there is always an incredibly long list of attributes, likes and dislikes that you have to go through. I suppose they are trying to match you with a soulmate. Or are they? Or is it just a con, only there to attract the lonely and vulnerable with the hope of finding the love of their life?

You need to persevere. No pain no gain, right? You have completed the questionnaire and now for the tricky bit: how to describe yourself? You want to appear as truthful as possible and engaging. It is tough. How do you sell yourself and remain genuine and without appearing too arrogant?

Obviously, you want to put your best side forward but, then again, remain as objective as possible because if this is going to work, you will need to be yourself and your new partner needs to like the real you.

You select the pictures to put online, pay the fee, complete the questionnaire, submit and wait to receive the OK from the moderator and you are good to go.

By then you have spent hours completing your profile with accuracy and hope that others have done the same. After all, you want to meet someone that matches your personality the most.

Here is what I came up with:

Vivacious and genuine

Possibly a bit too honest, I tend to wear my heart on my sleeve. Having said that, it's difficult to describe yourself whilst remaining objective and neutral. I suppose it comes with the territory but I like good food, some wines and I am passionate about the things I do.

I am affectionate, caring, loyal, expressive and genuine but most of all I am still an old-fashioned romantic who likes to be treated with respect. Not too sociable before my morning coffee, but worth knowing after that! I like to keep busy and active,

I keep fit at my gym throughout the year to enjoy my skiing to the full when the season comes.

I recently have gone back to doing the things I used to enjoy, from playing in an orchestra to singing as well as a bit of amdram too. I enjoy going to watch a play, movie, listen to live music (any type really), go out with friends or lose myself in a novel when I feel less sociable

As I am watching my daughters start their own lives, I feel it is also my time for me to reach new horizons and would love for someone to share that journey with me.

I selected a few RECENT pictures.

Three to be precise: one as I was going to the previous year's Christmas party; it was a posh affair so Ted Baker dress and heels. One close up from my last birthday celebration where I cropped out my daughters' faces from the picture. The final one from my last skiing holiday. I choose some of the better pictures, if there are such a thing, and one where I smiled as I wanted to stand out from the crowd.

Thinking that, without reading the profile, you can see what I look like, that I can look smart and that I am active and like skiing so that my reader could build a little mental image.

Before submitting your profile, you give a quick read of the safety pages. They may be stating the obvious, but always wise. No?

Naturally, you wish to maintain your privacy and avoid your identity to be stolen or avoid fraud, which doesn't just apply to online dating. You know that your identity is precious and that identity theft is on the rise, besides, you don't want to say everything online and keep something to say for your potential first date!

You know that chatting online is fun, but do you know who you are actually talking to? If you have children, you have already warned them about this. People online are not necessarily who they say they are nor what they seem to be. Unfortunately, that remains the case at any age.

You read all about how to connect with people online, and how to get to know them, but take your time and trust your instincts when communicating. It is wise to communicate via the site first as often the chats are monitored, and the same applies to what you have entered on your profile.

Dating sites, just like social networks and other internet services, are targeted by scammers. Scammers want one thing and one thing only: money. All sites give you examples of common scammer behaviours to watch out for and report. You could also end up being stalked and harassed. Cyberbullying is no joking matter at any age. You hear all the stories with youngsters about webcams: pictures that are sent by mistake to everyone, webcam conversations that are recorded and used to extort money.

We all know about these and by nature, dating online means that you will be online by default and fraudsters may use that and appeal to your better nature to help them out of an 'unfortunate situation' by sending money. They already know that you are alone and potentially vulnerable.

It goes without saying that money requests should be a red light and an absolute NO-NO. Yet some people still fall for it. Scammers will look to gain your sympathy with the stories they tell. It would be naive to assume scammers are illiterate foreigners that you and others will see through in an instant.

Scamming is a pretty sick line of business, but it is nevertheless a business for them. They practise tugging at heartstrings, at showing tenderness or a neediness. They know very well how to tell people what they want to hear. They are fraudsters and earn a living from it and are praying for our good nature.

I thought the various websites I registered on were treating me like a child when I read the advice to:

♥ Never give out bank account or other details;
♥ Beware of the sob story – someone telling you how much they want to visit you but need a loan to pay for the ticket/visas. Or stories about a desperately ill family member who needs help with medical expenses;
♥ The same goes for fantastic, too-good-to-be-the true business deal they are in on – if only they had some extra up-front money;
♥ Watch out for those profiles that immediately tug on the heartstrings – supposed ex-serviceman or woman – or those who claim to be recently widowed to gain your trust and sympathy;

- Our same warning goes for pleas of urgency – about money needed at short notice. Someone asking you to use a wire service to get money to them is up to no good;

- Be wary of long distance and overseas relationships: they can happen, but it is an unlikely way for a relationship to start offline so be wary online; and

- Notice if a contact seems out of touch or out of kilter: people offering foreign numbers for contact, people who seem not to be aware of things happening in the UK – events, the weather, etc. – people who want or need to send messages at unusual hours.

It goes with the territory, has if you are only online for any length of time you are bound to encounter some of those; it happened to me too.

Despite being warned about scammers, they are difficult to avoid, they are there. It is just a matter of keeping your cool, especially with quick declarations of love after only a few messages. If someone you are in contact with starts declaring their love for you within a matter of hours (or even days), it should definitely ring alarm bells.

The three scammers I encountered were textbook from the description given by the site. They would have had a far better chance of success if they had read the site guidelines and slightly diverteed from them!

I was about to report a scammer one day on a site, but someone else had already beaten me to it. The website advised me they had been removed for security purposes.

My scammers ticked at least three of the characteristics listed above and as a result, they were easily discovered.

To remain on the safer side of safe, you read all the safety advice on the website and follow the guidelines in respect of: choosing a username; completing your profile; protecting your personal information password and security; beware of accessing your account from a public space; you are careful about guidelines provided by the dating website.

You also have the opportunity to verify that the site you are using is a member of the Online Dating Association (ODA). Membership means that the site has to commit to an industry code of practice that includes honest communication with users, protecting their privacy and providing a mechanism for reporting abuse. The inclusion of the ODA's logo on the site indicates membership.

However, these people online are not checked for criminal records. You will often hear in the media about serious incidents following online dating. You can never be too careful, despite the fact that you could get a false sense of security because you're on a dating site, do your own research to learn more about someone and make an informed decision about meeting them or even continuing to chat to them.

You are also told to report unacceptable or suspicious behaviour. It goes without saying that you need to stop communicating with anyone who makes you feel uncomfortable or apprehensive. You should never feel embarrassed to report a problem to the dating service. You are helping them and doing other users a favour.

To pay or not to pay? That is also a question.

You need to balance the expensive membership with the size of the database. In terms of subscription, I believed that the more expensive a site, the more dedicated the men would be and perhaps more serious. Assuming that the free sites where literally everyone goes and register for a laugh. Some of my friends were on free dating websites and the profiles on there were, I was told, pretty dire.

I always tried the membership paying ones and followed the rating of the comparative website. You do it for car insurance, so why not for dating?

Site selected.

Profile completed.

Safety guideline digested.

Online dating here I come!

2
• • •

FROM THE SUBLIME
TO THE RIDICULOUS

Now that your profile has been published on your chosen website, you are ready to start your search. You have gained access to men's profiles and your adventure to find 'true love' is about to begin.

Of course, you are online to attract the attention of a potential partner and it is human nature to try to embellish a little of either your personality or your abilities, but sometimes it is just laughable. The content of the profiles you are confronted with tends to vary considerably from no picture, no description, nothing at all to the War and Peace description on just how wonderful they are illustrated with eleven photos. Profiles are all very different and yet the content is rarely original and at times barely comprehensible. OK, so it is not meant to be the highest level of literature, but surely you do not want to show yourself as being illiterate?

FIRST LOOK

The Pictures

I would say the first glance is probably the most important. Not that I am particularly shallow, but if I am to spend the rest of my life with that person, there needs to be a certain degree of attraction. Like in so many life situations: first impressions do matter.

Very few men are actually smiling on their pictures, as if the stern, serious, boring look sells. I will pass on the too dark, badly cropped, too bright, even the picture with sunglasses where you can't see anything. The ones who are not aware of the existence of selfies and feel that taking a picture in front of a mirror and uploading such a picture is actually enhancing their look. It isn't.

There should be a happy medium here; half-naked holiday snaps by the pool displaying your beer belly in its full glory may not be the side of you to show first. Sometimes, less is more! The same thing applies to photographs in budgie smugglers. I do not think it is the look to go for either for any age group. Also, best to avoid sunglasses or a hat, or both; it defeats the purpose if having a picture!

I am also passing on the pictures often sent later, as they wouldn't have been allowed by the site moderator, of a specific part of male's anatomy. What is generally referred to in the trade as a 'dick pic'. My first and only one was quite a shock – nothing to do with its size, unfortunately.

I was so surprised by it my usual quick wit and repartee dried away instantly. Sadly, my perfect comeback only came to me a few days later: "O*h, that looks like a penis, only smaller."* At least now I have the perfect answer for the next one I receive! I am still baffled how anyone can think that would make a good impression.

Uploading recent pictures is also advisable: I have seen a profile in 2015 with a picture of him dating from 1999! He even had the cheek of asking me if I still fitted in the dress I had on in my profile picture.

Indeed, my pictures were recent. One was actually a week old at the time of registration. They may not be all that flattering but at least mine would give my potential date a fair indication of what I look like now.

Posting a picture of a man + female, man + dog, cat or a fish or any sort of pet is to my mind not the best idea either. Neither is the picture taken with the best male mate(s) at the party as you don't know which of the two drunken louts you are messaging. You could end up going on a date, not with the guy you thought you were... or maybe that was the plan all along.

I came across the same photo, two different profiles in two different towns? Twins?

I also saw pictures of sunsets, a lamb in a field, horses, the head of a swan and what I thought to be a jellyfish but later stood corrected: it actually was a fossil. Why? What is the message being conveyed here? One big question remains: why have a picture of your car / motorbike / boat on your profile picture? Why the need to display your wealth?

You also find many pictures out of focus, the ones where it shows from the neck down to the top of the belly button – brilliant for the torso fetishist – and then you have the one who wants to make sure you have their last photo album. One guy had twenty-seven pictures on his profile which led me to sense an acute case of egocentricity.

Which picture and how many to choose?

It's complicated.

Or no pictures

52 – 6' European, non-smoker Christian, likes music, books and outdoors.

60 – Caucasian, Catholic non-smoker – likes to relax.

Surely, you would need a bit more than that to form an opinion and to consider engaging in a conversation?

Perhaps it is an indication of my potential lack of sense of adventure. But those are a bit vague. This would certainly not tease my female sense of curiosity.

It's complicated.

The AKA

Some sites will insist that you give yourself an AKA; not sure why, as you have the picture on sight anyway so I am not sure to what purpose.

Cute but articulate. Articulate, granted, but cute? Matter of opinion. No?

Manofkent. Original for a man from Kent. No? And there were quite a few!!

It's complicated.

People you recognise

One of the main disadvantages of uploading your pictures is that if you have a friend or colleague also online, they are going to recognise you and also see that you have looked at their profile. And vice versa.

My first ever experience, the first day, first ever search and the guy who appeared to be my match was someone from work. Oops.

Do you:

A) Swiftly get off his profile, hoping that he won't check later to see who has been viewing his profile, because if he does, he will see you! And will know that you have seen he is online, he knows you are single, online, and, horror, he may even think you secretly fancy him or that you may be an easy touch? Will he tell people at work?

B) Wink?

C) Send a message and if so, what kind of message? Would you consider going out with someone from work? Do you send an 'ah ha lol' type of message, isn't that funny? Look who the computer has matched me to. LOL.

The first time it happened to me, I knew the guy in question fairly well and we both knew we were on a dating site so we did talk online and continue to talk at work too as previously. But it made me think.

What is the correct protocol for this?

It's complicated. Not to mention potentially awkward. I happened to recognise other people I knew too.

One of them was a particular slap in the face as I quite liked the guy. I didn't know him all that well but he was good fun and we had previously organised to spend a weekend in Paris, which he had organised. It was a separate bedroom type of scenario. I automatically assumed that he was in a relationship and I forgot my original intentions and we had a fab weekend in Paris.

We stayed in touch for a number of years, but when I saw that he actually was single and dating online, it was not good for my ego. I suppose I am not irresistible and not everyone's cup of tea. Fair enough. But we had spent lots of time together, corresponded for a while so he must have liked my company, personality, etc… so what was wrong with me?

On a couple of occasions, I had received messages from someone living locally to me, one of which I had actually spotted on the high street, but it was a busy Saturday morning. Luckily, he didn't recognise me but to my horror ended up in the queue behind one of them at B&Q one day. We looked at each other; he was with someone else and I certainly wasn't going to say anything, but now wondered whether he recognised me with my old baggy tracksuit bottoms full of paint and a similar top. A slight change from the usual pictures I had put online. Surprisingly enough, I hadn't put any of me in full DIY gear!

In addition to the people from work and from another part of your life you recognise, there are also men that you have previously encountered when they were partners of someone you knew. It is always a little surprising when you go on a date and they admit knowing you. It is actually scary.

It happened to me a couple of times.

The first time, as it turned out we had been at the same places at the same time when he was still my friend's partner. Yet I couldn't remember. Then again, I do not look at my friends' partners and think, "Hehe, I call dibs for when the two of you split up."

We had started to chat online about rugby, the Six Nations or some other tournament must have been on at the time and as it happened it turned out to be something we had in common. We were happily chatting when I asked if he had any plans for the weekend and he said he was meeting friends who lived in a town nearby. I said I had a friend who lived there too. He asked who and I was very careful to only mention her shortened first name, as it was not that uncommon. I thought I was not divulging too much information. Telling that you know someone called Kate in London I thought would be pretty safe. "Oh, I know her," he answered back and I thought, "Of course you do."

A couple of weeks later, we met for lunch; it was a little difficult to recognise him as he didn't look anything like his picture, but we got there in the end and as it turned out, not only he did know my friends but most of the group of people I socialise with. He had been dating one of them for seven years!

Incredible!

The second time, I had been conversing with a pleasant enough guy online, then on the phone, one of our natters turned to what we did for a living. I told him what I did and who for and he asked, "Do you know X?"

"Indeed, I do. She is one of the managers at work."

"What a small world!"

Always is. At times you wish it wasn't so tiny!

We arranged a date, an evening meal, really nice meal actually, probably one of my better ones. It was all going well and he said:

"It's funny that you know X."

"Funny is not the word I would have chosen."

"Small world, no?"

"Indeed, how do you know her?

"We used to go out. Not very long, maybe a few months and a number of years ago."

"I see."

"I thought I'd tell you straight away."

"Honesty is always the better option."

"I hope you don't mind, but I asked her what type of person you were before I invited you on a date."

[*What? Of course, I bloody mind! How could I not*

enjoy being the source of potential idle gossip at work? Do you also intend to run a comparative study?]

"Not sure that she knows me that well outside of work."

"It was all good, don't worry."

"I am not too worried, we are both professionals and I do not think the topic of dates will ever come up in any of our conversations."

And it didn't.

"I am still in touch with her, maybe one day we can double date with her new boyfriend."

"I don't think that's going ever to happen."

Of course, if you become a seasoned online dater like me, you can easily recognise the disillusioned seasoned male online dater, who like you, is giving all possible dating sites a chance.

SECOND LOOK

The description

It is always a difficult task. How to describe yourself simply and accurately without boasting and also encouraging someone to make contact? It is a difficult task, granted, so perhaps a little thought about it may not be superfluous.

Some websites do assist you in giving a description of yourself by asking a series of questions such as: if you won the lottery what would you buy first? What would you take on a desert island, can't live without, etc? To the question, 'What is your most treasured possession?' it was noticed that the majority of men owned their children and happily put children as their prime possession.

One answered his haircut when he was bald. So bald and funny, amidst a load full of unoriginal answers, his answer had the merit of being entertaining and deserved one of my approving comments and generated a few discussions thereafter.

At the question, 'What do you do for fun?' it goes without saying that they all like to wine and dine. Unfortunately, this has a different meaning for different people: a guy questioned if I thought a fried chicken fast food chain was a suitable venue for a date. Fast food chains are definitely not in my definition of fine dining! He appeared to be put out when I ask if he was serious about fast food chain as a restaurant. He was!

It's complicated.

Likes and dislikes

Even if they live miles from the nearest coastline, many men like going out for a walk by the sea. I don't live too far from the sea myself and I must confess that on occasions, I have enjoyed driving to the coast and walking on the seafront. I must say that on these walks I have never ever seen any single man walking on their own, ever. They must have separate beaches just for them or I was just terribly unlucky not to ever see one.

They all like music; well, who wouldn't? There are enough genres that you are bound to like at least one type of music! I found that all kind of music tends to mean the type of music they listened to in their teenage years and for which they still have the LP for.

Besides jazz, there is very little I would switch to the next radio station for. I like everything from classical to pop, but whatever I listened to, I was told was rubbish. I went out with one of those who like ALL types of music, except for what I liked, and for the three months we went out together we only listen to the same album and often it was just the same song.

I also noticed that cycling became a very popular activity enjoyed by British men, possibly due to a few medals at the Olympics and the Tour de France coming to the UK (*another mystery: how can it be the Tour de France in Yorkshire?*) and the picture, with cycle shorts should be kept out of profiles too. Please.

All men online like to keep fit. Judging by some of the pictures and the extra pounds they carry, some probably consider holding a beer glass at their local pub or playing darts a keep fit activity and justify a description of 'average built'. As I found out, liking to keep fit is mere wishful thinking rather than doing any form of physical activity.

I went on a date once and questioned how he was keeping fit, what gym he belonged to, etc. to make conversation as his profile said he liked running and had run 10k for charity. It turned out that was seven years ago and hadn't put on a pair of trainers since.

Another 'fit' gentleman had put a picture of himself running a marathon which dated over fifteen years ago, and now didn't look anything like his profile picture! I had already forgotten that different people have different standards. Then again, I can understand the reluctance in saying, I do not usually go out, I am the biggest couch potato you have ever seen!

It's complicated.

What is not on the profile

It was very interesting to see what was missing from the profiles; no one ever said they like to spend time watching sports or staring at the football results for hours on end on a Saturday afternoon or that they were going to watch *Match of the Day* religiously every Saturday evening. Remarkable! Someone should contact the BBC to let them know that actually, no one watches the matches they put on and the replays.

Continuing on the fiction side of the profile, if you have lied about your age *(how vain are you?)*, or about your height or your weight *(a few extra pounds usually means you need two seats on the plane, very economical with the truth, the question is not how much would your ideal weight be?)*, you are going to be found out very quickly.

I suppose woman may be tempted to shave a few years, pounds even, from their profiles, one thing is certain: they are hardly going to lie about their height. So, when you have a Tom Cruise complex and have lied about your height on your profile, don't ask a woman taller than yourself on a date and, if you have, it is best to try to avoid the look of utter disappointment and disbelief when you get to greet her.

If you drink four bottles of beer, two bottles of wine and a little spirit on a daily basis and something a little stronger at the weekend, you are not a social drinker, the word you are looking for is 'alcoholic', but that category is not offered in the selection.

If you smoke close to two packets of cigarettes a day, you are neither a non-smoker nor genuinely trying to quit.

If you are born in Syria you are not Eastern European.

I also read, "I don't have attachments but I see my mum every evening." Very commendable, but this is by definition possibly the strongest attachment of all.

The status

Here again, the different standards are quite noticeable. The many discussions I have had with potential partners in respect of the status gave this book its name.

Those little chats more often than not resulted in an 'it's complicated' answer. So much so that I was wondering how stupid I must look. Would I really not be able to comprehend the situation? How complicated must it be?

The fact is, you would be able to understand, you just wouldn't like it. It's complicated in the sense that you want to know something he doesn't want to disclose.

In my early days of dating, I always gave the benefit of the doubt. Yes, it could be difficult or painful to talk about your circumstances and your (ex) wife or partner, but you quickly reach the conclusion that if you hear the "it's complicated" answer, there is, in fact, nothing difficult to understand, you just wouldn't like the answer. The situation is that he wants a little bit on the side and he doesn't want you nor his wife to find out. Nothing to do with my capacity of grasping a complex situation.

A fact of my online dating experience is the majority of men I met were double, even triple, dating if not still married or living with their partner. From personal experience, I would say that around two out of three of the men I talked to online were still in a relationship, which could be simply due to my age group.

It's complicated only meant, "I want my cake, the icing, the cherry on top of the icing and still eat that cake and, if at all possible, the other cakes on the stand." When found out, they will launch into the 'misunderstood' story and how unhappy they are and how they had stopped being intimate… to listen to them you could easily reach out for the tissues, but then realise that they'll never leave that situation either and that it is only an act to soften you.

In the end, it only makes you more and more cynical.

I encountered those more often than I would have liked. It hadn't been as upsetting as someone I knew of, who had been for years and years with a man who was living a double life and played the happy carefree boyfriend with her, while also playing the married husband with two kids with another woman. She eventually found out ten to twelve years on and eventually told people when breaking down at the question, do you have children?

I had the misfortune to get briefly caught by a similar gentleman. He was intelligent, well-groomed, funny, good-looking and excellent company. What more could I want? I felt really happy I had found such a great guy and was blissfully going out with him until I found out a little snag: he was still married.

One day, as we were together, his wife rang him and I saw a real look of fear in his eyes. "Oh my God," he said. "She almost found out about us." I thought he was going to say, "Oh my God! You have found out I was married." But no, my feelings were not even briefly considered. It was clearly my cue to leave. He pleaded, said I got it all wrong. They were still married, but there was nothing there. According to his story, he and his wife were no longer intimate and it was more or less over. At the time, I wasn't sure whether to believe him or not. The sure thing was, I didn't want any part of it.

A few months later, quite by chance, I found out that his wife was expecting a child. It didn't take Einstein to work out that this child had been conceived whilst he was busy with me and when, according to him, they were no longer intimate. I made a point of re-contacting him and advised him to get a DNA test, as either he was related to Pinocchio or this child wasn't his.

It's complicated.

Divorced

My definition of divorced is when somewhere in your paperwork you are in possession of a Decree Absolute granted by a court. If you haven't got it, you are not divorced and you are still legally attached to someone else. It is that simple.

Unfortunately, only lawyers and I share that view. Your wife moving away with her new boyfriend is not a divorce especially if you are desperate to get her back. It doesn't matter how long ago she has moved away, without a Decree Absolute you are still legally bound.

It may be just a simple piece of paper and means nothing, but I believe it is problematic to start and build a long-lasting relationship when the last one is still not completely dissolved.

It's complicated.

Never married

Usually straightforward.

However, if you are still living with the mother of your children, whether married or not, it is pretty much the same as being married.

Similarly, if you are still living with your parents at the tender age of fifty-five and you are not caring for them, it is a little awkward. I wouldn't dream of replacing your mummy.

It's complicated.

Widowers

I was also contacted by widowers. As sad as their situation may be, they also need to find romance and rebuild their lives. I have a lot of sympathy for them. It is so tough to let go of someone you love.

A widower contacted me once, very nice prose, sweet, sensitive and candid. He revealed that after a long battle with cancer his wife had passed away a few years previously and that he felt he was ready to rebuild his life. He went on saying that he liked my profile and asked me a few questions to which I felt compelled to answer.

Unfortunately, his entire conversations were about his late wife: where she liked to go on holiday, what she liked to do, how they spent their time together, etc. Every new message was a little more info about her, despite my endeavour to move to hobbies, plans for next weekend, next holidays, etc. It was heartbreaking. I kept on answering despite the fact that I knew he wasn't ready to move on, but I couldn't bring myself to tell him and waited until he realised and stopped messaging me.

It's complicated.

Separated

Always my favourite status. The subtitle of separated should be: avoid AVOID **AVOID!**

Over the years, I didn't even bother reading the 'separated' profiles nor answering the first email. If the status said separated, don't go there. Not even with a barge pole! Nine times out of ten it's only a wishful thinking and often translates to, "I have had a row with my wife and I slept on the sofa last night."

One had said, "I separated with my wife last week."*[please don't bother me, grieve and let me be.]* A lot of them are 'separated' but still live with their wives /

partners and talking to many of these guys, I would put money on the fact that the wives were not aware of the said separation.

Another reason to avoid the "separated" man is that more often than not the ex-wife or ex-partner is still pretty much a constant in his life. Unfortunately, at our time of life, our potential partner has a past. Whereas having a past is a given, it is a problem when the past is not quite past and pretty much part of the present too.

My sister told me a story of her friends who went on a date with a man and during the meal the phone rang; it was the ex-wife, her toilet was blocked and he left the restaurant mid-meal and the poor girl was left there to finish her meal and her date on her own.

The given answer for this kind of behaviour is, "She is the mother of my children," and generally that means and she whistles, he comes running. Not a particularly attractive trait or totally conducive for a start of a new relationship. The past is the past, but that looks dangerously like a future too.

You often end up baffled by that behaviour when said mother is actually the one who left the husband to be with someone else. You can only wish the children don't grow up with that kind of morals!

I met a guy who told me on the first date, "There is going to be three of us in the relationship. And the third person is my ex." He did say it on the first date and I was warned. I am not going to lie, I am not sure these dating tactics work. It certainly made him less of a catch very quickly.

Apparently, many of his previous relationships had broken up because of that. Who would have thought? He proudly announced that the ex made their lives miserable and continued way beyond their separation. After admitting to me that this had ruined his new relationships, I couldn't understand his unwillingness to change anything.

I would say not to get involved with a man who is still legally, possibly financially and even emotionally involved with his ex. If they haven't taken the step to divorce, time told me not to touch with a barge pole; I got that particular T-shirt once.

It's complicated.

Children

This should generate a straightforward answer: you either have some or not. At the question, 'Do you want children?' some would answer, 'Yes at some point'. Is it really what you want or what you feel you should answer if you are over 60? It makes you look as if you are hedging your bets.

One of my friends went on a date, which she said had gone rather well. At the end of the date, she suggested meeting the following Sunday for lunch, to which he answered, "I can't next Sunday; I see my sons playing football."

Sons… sons? What sons? From memory, she thought the profile hadn't mentioned any children at all and went straight back on the profile to check… no, no children there. Under children, the answer was, "None." Little cherubs, they do grow up so quickly!

I corresponded and later met a guy, father of 3 who had only put 1 child on his profile. Clearly, the other two were not important enough to deserve a mention.

It's complicated.

Limited information

Some profiles only divulge a Christian name or an AKA, age, location (of course the computer gives this as soon as you have registered. Then the only entry made by the guy is one word or just a three-word sentence.

How could you possibly start a conversation if the profile only has the name (which is probably an AKA), an age and a location and possibly one adjective?

The system automatically prompts you to 'request a picture from Rob' and highlights the link for you to click to request a picture. Clearly, if Rob couldn't spare two minutes to upload a photo and the very basic of information, how likely is he to answer your email? Make contact? Read your profile? Meet you?

It's complicated.

Alcohol

This is quite an interesting topic as different people have different standards. Me, I get really sick after three glasses of wine; I drink wine usually to complement my food and don't see the point of drinking to get 'wasted'.

I very much enjoy being merry but not so much the hangover the next day, so I have learned from previous mistakes and leave it at a reasonable consumption level.

Other people clearly have different standards. There is one thing I learned during my online dating days: going on a date with someone who drinks to the point of not standing up is not fun.

When I was toying with the idea of writing about my online dating experiences, I watched a Polish movie during a long-haul flight on the very topic. Two people who met online met for a drink. The guy ordered two double vodkas and then looked at the girl who said, "Oh I don't drink," and the guy repeated to the waitress, "Two double vodkas and an orange juice for the lady, please." And the drinking went on. It made me laugh out loud as unfortunately, I did encounter gentlemen like that.

The result of being 'wasted' is not always savoury.

But more on my personal experiences later.

It's complicated.

Or too much information

Some will tell you the ins and outs of their lives, a copious amount of irrelevant information and even disclose their income.

It's complicated.

Genuine and easy going

If I had £1 each time I saw the word 'genuine' or 'easy going' I would have stopped working by now. Apparently, all men are genuine, even the married ones! Genuinely looking for a bit on the side! I met such an easy-going kinda guy during my time online and my definition of easy-going and his were vastly different.

Most of them are very honest and hard-working, even the ones who give you their work email address to message you out of sight because it is 'easier at work'. Interesting work ethics!

It's complicated.

Romantic

Some sites can ask you if you are romantic, very romantic or not romantic at all.

Based on my personal experience, I would say that the vast majority of the men online wouldn't know romantic if it was wearing red flashing neon lights and hitting them with a baseball bat. Yet in all their profiles, they happily stated that they are either 'romantic' or 'very romantic'. Even the ones seeking a little on the side! To my mind, these options were chosen to lure the unsuspected lady to message. Or we have vastly different meanings for the word romance.

It's complicated.

If you had one wish?

The one wish for the majority of guys would be world peace. Really? That answer was so common I thought I had been time-warped into the Miss World contest.

Luckily, some were more realistic with their wish: *"West Ham to win the Champions League."* At least this had the advantage of being funny.

Similar with: *"Endless supply of Somerset cider."*

Some men can't count to one. The one wish was, *"Health and fitness, true love, a house by the sea, a daily walk on the beach and (of course) world peace."* I made that six wishes.

On occasions, some of the answers caught my attention because they were either original or funny and prompted me to start messaging. I remember thinking at the time that it was a great way to get someone's attention and starting a conversation. Alas, it didn't happen often enough. Lack of imagination seemed to prevail.

One had said he would wish to have a superpower. Naturally, this provoked my sense of curiosity and encouraged me to ask what superpower would that be? To which he answered along the lines of using the powers for good and not evil and with it demonstrated a complete lack of imagination and wasn't even the answer to my question. He concluded his paragraph asking me what I would choose. Me? Easy, I would like to become invisible; there are so many situations where I would love to be a fly on the wall. His reply came, "Ah yeah, good one." And that became the end of our encounter.

Another one had answered, *"I would like to be able to write in the clouds."* How poetic, I thought. Once again it prompted me to enquire: "What words of wisdom would you write in the clouds for us to see?" The answer didn't have the same appeal: "Build more bridges." On second thought, I thought it could have been an excellent metaphor. Sadly, it wasn't. He mentioned he was referring to the bridge like the one between Denmark and Sweden. I was at a loss for a response. I clearly put far too much thought into his answer.

It's complicated.

The pseudo philosopher

"You can't change yesterday and only today as tomorrow will always be tomorrow."

"You need to let people be whoever they are."

It's complicated.

The poet

Of course, there are also the wannabe poets out there, who feel the need to share their verses with you.

One such gentleman actually wrote a few verses for me. I wasn't sure what to think about them. Verses yes, however, not terribly meaningful, more like a few words put next to each other with not a lot of meaning, nor evoking anything really.

It's complicated.

Some of my most memorable descriptions

"I have a son who I love very much." Not exactly ground-breaking news. But that sentence came up fourteen times in the profile. Maybe a little psychotic? Next.

"Any woman who uses her children as weapons or holds a man responsible for her happiness is 'entirely' not my type. Hope that's clear!" What's clear is that you are not quite over your ex. Not with a barge pole! Next.

"*I dislike vagabonds.*" ??? Next.

"*I enjoy scented candles.*" Seriously? Next.

"*I am loyal to my staff.*" Great! Is the position of girlfriend still vacant? Next.

"*Professionally I am ambitious, driven, decisive, good at managing people and highly efficient and organised.*" Sorry, you are on the wrong site, this is dating! I didn't want your CV. Next.

"*I am well travelled and knowledgeable about a wide range of things.*" Modest and humble with it. Next.

"*I have been to forty-eight countries.*" Happy for you. Next.

"*I enjoy watching Bollywood movies.*" Actually not such a useless piece of information, but I don't. So next.

"*Resistance and a sense of duty are essential to me.*" And that's the first thing you want to put on your profile? Next.

"*I do not want a bad woman.*" Really? That comment is sure to scare all the bad ones away. Next.

"*I don't like bunny boilers.*" I am not sure that many people do. Next.

"*I do not expect a woman to engage in a relationship with me for money!*" That is undoubtedly going to discourage all the gold diggers out there! Next [*not that I am a gold digger but that sounds too weird for me!*].

"*I am genuine what you is what you get.*" So someone who didn't take the time to review what he has written and who didn't realise a word was missing. Slapdash and approximate then. Next.

"I like to keep my household tidy." Very commendable, but I don't need a cleaner. Next.

"Whether it be family life a sport or a master just to name a few." Interesting conversation ahead. Don't even understand the opening sentence of the profile. Next.

"I have lived in many countries and enjoy lunch and dinner." Difficult to resist such a specific insight into a life. Next.

"I like good food and wine." Isn't that a waste of characters from the 500 needed for your description? Next.

"I am a lover of wine." Possibly alcoholic? Next.

"In my spare time, I like to fly my helicopter." I had to ask whether it was a real one or a toy one. It was a real one. As the Beatles sang: 'Can't buy me love' sadly. Next.

"I am a very structured person and like everything to follow an orderly path." Fun fun fun! Next.

"I like to pay clear attention to balance and harmony." Meaning? Next.

"Very attentive, considerate and caring." Yet single; I fear you may not be telling everything. Next.

"In order to achieve what I want I need people who stand behind me and support me." Needy, then. Next.

"I work hard, as my dream won't work unless I do." Am I part of that dream? Next.

"They should know that I am creative twenty-four hours a day." Good for you, who is they? Next.

And I have kept the best till last:

"Not brilliant in bed but can say lovely things when it goes wrong." NEXT!

Interesting answers

Things you couldn't do without: *"My kids."* Well sure, but the question said 'things.'

A few words to describe yourself: *"I am your friend."* Mmmm a little creepy maybe?

What is important to you? *"Not scuffing my alloy wheels."* Not sure what to say, is this really what will help you find love?

"Intelligent, attractive, interesting and humble." Obviously humble and modest with it.

"I like a woman who takes care of her appearance / herself." Quite a common statement, to tell the truth. Funnily enough, I believe women also like a man who is decently groomed.

What are you grateful for? My love of music.

What are you passionate about? Travelling. Will ensure my passport is renewed.

What is your best feature? Always their bum, happily taking their word for it, you really don't want to go there.

One said being a dad, in case you were going for a father figure.

What are you looking for in a relationship? Friendship. Seriously, there's no point paying a subscription to a dating website if you just want a friend. Surely you can start the hobby you always wanted to do, choir, orchestra or learn a new language etc. At least there you are sure to meet a friend with a common interest.

"Do you know what you are truly looking for until you have found it?" Someone passes me a bucket, please.

"The final piece of the jigsaw to complement their lives." Isn't that just a little self-centreed? As well as demonstrating your poor command of your own language.

"Lots of sex." Honest.

Where do you feel most at home? *"Nudist beach."* At last, a sense of humour!

It's complicated.

3

• • •

MESSAGING

Since this is your first contact with a new person and potential life-long partner, perhaps a little thought is required.

As with any other forms of communication, first impressions do matter. This is with the understanding that, if you contacted someone, you would expect a reply. So, the first message is, to my mind, to engage in a dialogue and start to know each other.

To make things easier, the message should end with a question so as to encourage a response and further exchanges. If a question is too direct then leave the last sentence open-ended in the hope of keeping the messages flowing.

Generally speaking, I very rarely sent the first message for the simple reason that I didn't want to appear desperate and I would much rather be the chosen one than being the chaser. Besides, that technique has the added benefit of saving me agonising over what to say in that all-important first email.

If the profile was interesting and gave out a special vibe, I may have been inclined to send a smile or a wink or perhaps say what I liked in the profile. Which, on occasions, led me to have a few chats with people I would never have spoken to in my usual course of my life. That was the highlight of online dating.

Sadly, more often than not, you opened your inbox and stumbled upon a pointless message and felt a real sense of disappointment. You got advised by email that you had a message and you realised that it was just one word or complete gibberish.

As a rule, I never responded to monosyllabic first contacts either: hi, nice, hey, etc. Quite frankly, if you can't be bothered to make the first approach a decent one, you are not really that motivated. You are always told that the first impression is always the ones that last, so if you can only manage 'hi' then it is 'bye' from me.

The same applied to the guy who sends

'Hi' on the 7th of the month – no answer from me.

'Hello' on the 15th of the month. Still not warranting an answer from me. I could have suggested a different approach since the two first ones were unsuccessful. I didn't.

'Hello, how are you?' on the 20th. Still wasn't tempted to answer.

'Hello' again on the 29th. Ten out of ten for persevering, but quite honestly if I didn't answer the first time, what on earth made him think that I would the next three times?

Desperation?

It's similar with guys who will start by asking you exactly what appears in the first line of your profile. Demonstrating that they only looked at the picture, or just didn't look at all and tried their luck. Sorry, but that is not good enough.

On the opposite side of that coin, some will send you full details of their life story and you think, hang on a minute, aren't you just rehashing your profile here? It helps if the message received actually ends in a question to get the conversation going. Those sort of close-ended sentences do not encourage you to answer and sometimes you don't even know what you could possibly answer.

It's complicated.

Sex on the first message?

Not sure if that is the best introduction! Does it get any answers? It certainly didn't work for me. Especially when said gentleman was seriously out of shape. He chose to start straight on with sexual preferences. Interesting. Maybe he didn't have anything better to say and a better idea of how to present himself. Or maybe I was simply on the wrong website.

One of my first message from a guy was, "Hello there, do you fancy a FWB?"

I had to answer that one as I was intrigued and wanted to know what FWB was. "FWB?" I typed back. It didn't matter how ignorant that must have looked, I was curious.

Him: "Friends With Benefits."

Of course, silly me.

I have many friends, usually kind, generous, reliable, dependable, funny, intelligent, which is already remarkable, some I have known since I was seven or twelve years old and certainly never been any 'benefits'. Always thought the 'benefits' were best kept for a unique person where you have another kind of feelings for.

So that day I learned what FWB meant. They do say you learn something every day. What they do not mention is how useful that knowledge is! On that occasion, it wasn't.

This particular encounter did not end there. I was telling the FWB story to one of my friends, also dating online and she said she had the same thing. I showed her the picture of my hopeful contender and funnily enough, it was the same guy who had sent her the same message. My friend is easily twenty years younger than me. I felt privileged. But I couldn't help wondering, does it actually work? How many messages like that does he send in one day? What was his success rate?

I was also told once: "Come on a date with me and later we can continue somewhere where I can give you lots of organisms." Another moment of genuinely Laughing Out Loud for me.

My text back said: "Organisms? Are you sure?" He was indeed pretty sure and there were plenty of those available. I sadly declined the generous offer it wasn't all that appealing after all. I certainly did not want to catch any of those organisms!

A friend of mine had told me that, in her experience, sex was expected on the second date. It certainly hadn't been my experience at all and I wasn't sure whether to be pleased or offended by this. Sex on the first message is actually an excellent way to find out the ultimate motive of your potential date and save you a fair amount of time of wasted messaging. It was a definite no no for me and the only 'sure thing' was to move on to the next profile.

The first message is also where the full horror of the texting language comes out, coupled with bad grammar and single letter spelling:

"its the blu dress that court my eye."

"Do u want a fella." Difficult to resist such an invitation! But I did.

Once I had the following message: *"I no u there not but yr the home side."*

It was impossible to find the correct words to answer. As it was during the Euros in 2016, I was guessing he was referring to football, but I couldn't be sure and left it at that. No point in engaging a conversation with that one, being online is time-consuming enough, but a lot worse if you have to qualify as a cryptographer.

I had a long message once.

Very long.

I was intrigued as the profile stated that he was living near the town my parents grew up in France and yet the profile was in English. The first message was pleasant and I answered. I asked him if he still lived in France.

"No," he replied. "I lived in Ireland."

I double checked the town in the profile and it definitely was a town in France and not in Ireland. I thought it was odd to have a different town that your actual one on your profile and it would complicate the actual get-together dating part of the process, but after a few months online, nothing surprises you.

After just a couple of exchange of emails, he gave me his mobile phone number and his full name to be able to find him on a professional social network and his professional phone number. I was a little surprised; since he lived in a different country I was unlikely to ring him and organise an introduction, professional or otherwise.

I hadn't even thought of an answer to the last email I received from him, than I received another one from him saying he didn't want to continue messaging as we lived in different countries. He added that this couldn't lead to anything as he lived too far. Well, I hadn't moved house in between him sending his first two emails. Surely, he knew I lived in a different country BEFORE he started sending me all the details and starting to talk to me.

It's complicated.

Where is the logic in that?

Along the lines of 'I am on a dating website but have decided not to date', there are other kinds of completely illogical behaviours, not atypical, but certainly illogical.

For people who have never had the joy of online dating, when you are on a site, your profile is seen by many many people. It is the purpose of the game, after all. Someone will eventually like the look and sound of you and will want to know more. This will hopefully lead to a date and if the chemistry is there, you may become one of the success stories the sites are keen to promote.

Men do look at your profile and you can see that. All sites offer the possibility of deleting profiles of people you don't wish to have there, or block / report people if you feel that there is a problem or a safety issue. Every now and then you have one of your viewers who viewed you, every day, sent you a wink, or any other signs allowed by the site to show he has looked at your profile and liked what he saw.

Again, I am very old fashioned in that sense. Winking at me is certainly not going to make me think that you have put a lot of thought into this or that you are genuinely interested. If the only thing you can master is a virtual wink and hope for the best, it is not totally encouraging.

Truth be told, a real wink wouldn't have been much more successful either.

But the most entertaining is, when they have looked at / winked etc for a while without getting an answer back, they think that giving you their phone number is going to be the very thing you wanted. Sometimes they even give you their home phone number and may add that they are leaving the site. So please ring me, with no further words of encouragement.

If I understand the logic correctly, he was online for weeks, not saying a word, not messaging, just looking at the profile and winking from time to time, and at the very last minute, he gave his phone number and hoped for the best? Where is the logic in that?

Did they think that the thought of not having the occasional wink from someone who can't even start messaging would lead you to make a phone call?

It's complicated.

Can't you read?

I feel I also need to give a quick mention to the guys who try to start up a conversation and can't even copy my name correctly. In these cases, there is little to say. I felt that if they were unable or incapable of copying a few letters correctly, there is little point in answering, as they probably couldn't comprehend my answer anyway.

It's complicated.

Re-tired

Once I had a few messages from a retired guy. I was home one evening when his latest message was received and answered straightaway, hoping for a chat that evening.

Instead, it went all quiet for a couple of days and then the conversation resumed one evening. We were happily exchanging emails when he said, "Sorry to interrupt such a lovely conversation, but I need to pick up my friend from Heathrow. I'll be back in touch afterward as soon as I get back." Poor guy must still be there because it was the last I heard from him!

A few weeks later, I was cleaning up my online history on my phone, seeing a profile then deleting it so as to never have the person coming up on my search again and that retired gentleman came up and instead of swiping delete I clicked on a wink. Oops.

To which he answered, "Hello, how are you?" and I said, "Sorry, winked in error, it was meant to be 'delete'. Trust me, an easy mistake to make." Apparently, there was no need for that *[no need for honesty?]* as he was still keen to know more about me. He could have fooled me.

He messaged me the next day and fished by saying, "I have been up late last night and up early this am." *[Snap! I also commuted to work and did my eight hours before logging on.]* "My eyes are hardly staying open, it is almost painful." *[I get it, you are tired, you have had a busy day, of course, otherwise how could you justify such tiredness after one short night; the day must have been one hell of a day!]* He went on, "Please do not think I am trying to cut you off." *[That's exactly what I think you are doing, although in a roundabout way!]* He added, "I hope to speak properly soon, good night xxx"

Clearly not the case, as he never got in touch again. Although, it is worth mentioning that the message explaining why he couldn't message and how tired he was, was in itself a huge paragraph. But why bother? Wouldn't it have been simpler to just say, "I am not interested, let's leave it at that."

It's complicated.

Amazed

"How someone as beautiful as you can be on a dating website?" Good start, I thought, flattery, but heyho, he is dating and hopeful. I accepted the compliment and thanked him. And that was it, never heard from him again.

After a few weeks, I felt the need to send him a message. "Do you want to know why a girl as beautiful as I am on a dating website? It's because of people like you. So attractive and yet no one is asking me on a date so will remain beautiful and single forever."

His answer came two days later... "Would you like me to take you out?" So spontaneous it was difficult not to jump at the offer. I no longer felt beautiful, no thanks.

It's complicated.

"Hi, you look amazing, you're very attractive, good luck with this match thing, avoid the weirdos and the nutters."

I intend to, by not answering you.

How blonde do I look?

I had been messaging someone for a few days, possibly a couple of weeks. He sounded nice. He had his own business, three kids, all in their late teens. All seemed very normal and we had agreed to meet for a drink the following week.

Things were going well as far as messaging, texting and phone calls went and we were ready for the next step. At least I was. We had agreed a time and a place and I was genuinely looking forward to our first date.

The date day arrived and to ensure that time flew by, I had agreed to meet a friend during the afternoon for a shopping trip and she suggested we should grab a bite to eat before we parted. As we were roughly an hour prior to our meeting time, I sent a quick message to my date confirming that we were still meeting for a drink and that no food was involved. I just had dinner. He said it was just a drink, he was going to have dinner with his children before going out. It was all good.

My dinner came to an end and I was making my way to the rendezvous place we had agreed upon when I received a message: "I am not feeling well at all. Have just rung emergency doctor to come and visit."

"I hope it is nothing serious," I answered, concerned. "Let me know how you get on."

With that information, I decided to make my way home rather than to where we had agreed to meet. Fifteen, twenty minutes later another message came through.

"Really unwell, the doctor just leaving *[you have a doctor that comes out that time of night within fifteen minutes?]*, my blood pressure is through the roof." He even qualified his message by giving me the reading. Possibly hoping to cause a different reaction from me.

Not ever having had any problems with my blood pressure, I was unable to tell just how bad it was. Apparently, very.

He added, "I don't think I should get out of bed, I am not really up to it."

"Sorry to hear that, hope you get better soon," I replied, not wanting to show my disappointment.

I did consider asking him to let me know how he was getting on and potentially offer to re-schedule, but by that time, I had been dating online for a while and thought if he is ill and really wants to meet me, he'll soon contact me without me having to remind him. No need for me to patronise him into doing so. Besides, I rarely heard of ailments that go from fine to I can't move in under an hour. Then again, I am not a doctor.

Anyway, I was comforted by the fact that I had been warned on time. Cancellation at the last minute is one thing, being stood up quite another!

I was home and decided to go online and check my inbox for any winks, for potential suitors or someone who may have favourited me during the day. As I logged on, the latest messages and profile I had viewed, which happened to be my very nearly date, came up on my screen with a little pop-up message telling me that he was updating his pictures. At this very moment in time updating his pictures, when I was told just how poorly he was.

Bless! So ill and yet thought that the best way to recover was to update his profile pictures. People say that men cannot multitask! In true dedication to the search for love: even on his deathbed, he was still updating his pictures!

That was probably the cynical me talking, but I have had a few other excuses which are also worth a mention.

"*Sorry I can't make tonight, I have to do my VAT return.*" [And I thought you said you had an accountant, not a very good one, may I be so bold as suggesting you should find another one?

"*Sorry something has come up my nan has been taken to the hospital and I'll spend tonight with her.*" I would have felt sorry for him if he hadn't changed his profile pictures that very evening too. I didn't think you could use mobile phones in hospitals.

"*Sorry I forgot I was going to have lunch with my nan, I am very close to her, she'd be upset.*" If you were that close not sure you would have forgotten lunch with her.

It's complicated.

The online stalker

Unfortunately, online stalking happens rather a lot across all websites I have been on. You can see who has been looking at your profile during the day and as a result, the online stalkers are easily identifiable.

To tell the truth, this was my MO. Although not looking at the same profile over and over again but rather a little curious glimpse to show that I could be interested in knowing a little more. Only one look though, if nothing came out of it, I would certainly not repeat the experience. I wouldn't want to appear desperate or give an unsuspected soul the feeling that he was irresistible.

This seemed to be an easier way to kick the ball rolling, without having to agonise over what to say in that all-important first message. He would see that I had looked and then the ball is in his camp and he could either start a conversation or not. It did work; if they were interested, they soon made contact, if not, well then there is no point in insisting. What I did not do is look one day then again, the next and the next and the next. Sadly, many men did not understand that it could be borderline creepy.

It's complicated.

My wife left me

One of my first messages was from a guy from the same county, whose profile looked nice enough. He started to communicate that there were no reasons not to answer, and I did answer, which prompted him to pour his sorrows unto me.

His wife had been having an affair behind his back and he was devastated. Although very sad, it is not that unusual after all and it may be worth bearing in mind that there are always two sides to any stories. As I understood from his messages, his wife was unfaithful and she decided to leave him and move with her new man in another country and take the children with her too.

Double slap in the face. Although I did find it a bit extreme, leaving your husband because you are unhappy is quite common, having an affair still very common, but emigrating with the kids to join a stranger and separate your kids from their father is a bit extreme. Anyhow, the poor man never saw it coming and was pretty down. Within the third email exchange, he gave me his home number, as he said it would be good to talk to someone.

His home phone number? Seriously? Yes. Clearly, he wasn't as streetwise as he should have been.

Nobody had warned him that you never know who you meet online, it goes for the thirteen-year-old girl going online for the first time, the more mature woman dating online but also men. I am sure there are also female scammers out there and a fair amount of gold diggers. Anyway, I became the proud owner of his home phone number but was a bit concerned about it. Indeed, it is good to talk, but judging from previous email exchanges, he needed a counsellor far more than a potential partner.

Being the busy bee that I am, weekday evenings are not good for me. I go to orchestra and choir practice most weeks and even join in and assist some local drama productions. At times, I find it hard to remain in touch with my friends. Besides which, I also like going out for a drink with friends too. Anyway, ringing on a weekday evening was not the best idea, especially since I didn't feel it was going to be to arrange a date.

Two days had passed and I received an email asking me why I hadn't rung. I may be single but not sad, lonely nor desperate. I still have plenty in my life and spending my evenings by the phone is not an option. It can feel extremely lonely to be home alone, so I filled my evening as much as I could to meet and talk to people.

I know that it may seem that I may not have much time left for dating, which would be a fair comment, however, my life choices still gave me plenty of options if I decided to go on a date. I was actually freer and more available than when my girls were younger. If you really want to meet someone, you can easily miss the occasional practice without too much organisation. When your children are young, going out is much more of a task. As much as I enjoy my hobbies, they are still pretty easy-going activities, enabling me to have still many free evenings.

Anyway, back to my email, where I did explain in the nicest possible way that as it stated on my profile, *[which you may or may not have read prior to contacting me, but clearly should have]* that I led an active life with hobbies and friends to go out with it and that I am rarely home in the evenings, nor am I available to chat. Besides, I much prefer the company of others and meeting people face to face if at all possible.

He very much took umbrage to my explanation. I was as kind and sensitive as I could. I certainly didn't say that in this instance, I wasn't prepared to drop an activity just to hear him sob about his nasty, heartless wife. I had already read his emails which spoke of little else and I got that message loud and clear. The little contact we had hadn't convinced me he was ready to start a new relationship.

His last email telling me of his disappointment ended our communication, which was the best move since he didn't seem to appreciate me going out. I knew I wasn't the best person to assist him with his grieving and I moved on and left it at that. Coming up to five months later, I was still on the same dating website as I had paid for six months, *[no expense spared to find true love!]*, when he contacted me again. I answered.

I originally thought that he was better and giving me an update, but no. Then I received his second email, exactly the same as the second email five months previously. Copy and paste exercise.

"My wife was cheating on me behind my back and took the kids and emigrated with her new man."

Before he had a chance to throw his home phone number at me again, I reminded him that we already had this conversation a few months ago and that I still hadn't change my mind about staying home to specifically ring him. To be honest, we all have problems and I know it is very nice to share the with someone else and find a sympathetic shoulder to cry on, but not before you have actually met.

What amused me, in that case, was that I hadn't amended my profile or changed my picture or anything – it was exactly the same – but the guy had completely forgotten he had already spoken to me five months ago.

It's complicated.

Left on good terms

I had become a little disheartened by a specific website and had convinced myself to try out a new one. I had seen the advert on the television and thought, "Why not give that one a go?"

In those days, I believed that the quality of members would perhaps depend on the website.

Once again, the computer had matched me with someone I really didn't think was a match. As usual, I only found that out after reading the profile. I read the profile and left it at that, but he contacted me. During that short-lived membership on the site, I received a couple of long messages from him. The conversation wasn't all that riveting, it was about him, his DIY, his friends, etc. I can't remember him ever asking me any questions. What made me answer his first message was his profile which had amused me. He had described, at length, and by that, I mean at length, almost to the extent of knowing what he had for breakfast.

This is unusual as the majority of profiles where they are 'just genuine loyal kind of guy, who likes good food, good DVD with GSOH and who is looking for love' with very little else. In his profile, he had also described his ideal woman: petite, with brown hair, blue eyes, no more than size eight etc. I thought a little specific if you ask me, but who am I to judge? What also surprised me is how the computer algorithm came up with the conclusion that we were a match.

Anyway, he started to talk. I re-read his profile and the physical attributes of his perfect match, funnily enough possibly the exact opposite of what I look like. I couldn't help wondering, why was he writing to me? Hasn't he seen my pictures? Had he actually read my profile?

In his messages, he also went at length explaining to me that you could be friends with the opposite sex, which I very much agree with. I didn't need convincing. His emails were infrequent but very long when they were there. I answered occasionally and light-heartedly as I really didn't think we were ever going to meet.

As I had taken the decision to move on to another site I said my goodbyes and he gave me his email address. I thought, why not? What's the harm in that?

A few weeks later, I went on to register with another website and did a quick search on new members and funnily enough, his profile turned up. I felt compelled to send a little note saying, "No wonder, your messages were so infrequent, you are dating on two different websites, you must be a very busy boy."

His response was humorous: "I was just talking to your twin sister on another site and she was a lot more fun than you!" It made me smile and we carried on chatting.

He told me that he and his girlfriend had split up but in very amicable terms and that they were still living together. I was very surprised, to say the least.

"We left on good terms," he said, "and we have become good friends, there can be such friendship you know."

How can you still live under the same roof as your ex-partner and believe you can start something new? I couldn't understand why you would put yourself, your ex-girlfriend and the next one in such an awkward situation.

I was starting to become increasingly angry at these men who have absolutely no consideration for anyone else but themselves and I said bluntly, "Still living with your ex and dating, that is going to extremely interesting when you bring a girl home. I can imagine the tête-à-tête at the breakfast table. Ex and new girlfriend sharing a note and swapping little tales. That should be interesting!"

An abusive message came back where I was told I was the one not seeing the situation clearly. I didn't see the point in answering. I clearly saw he was heading for troubles and didn't want any part of that mess. He was the one on two different websites and still living 'in a different bedroom' with his partner. To my mind, not a situation conducive to the best start of your new relationship. It still makes me smile today to think that in that story, I was the one slightly warped.

A few months had passed when I received an email from him – almost an apology, one day in my inbox. He said that I was right and he had been extremely naive [*you don't say*] and I read on. He had a chat with his 'ex' and she didn't even think they were split up at all! She just saw it as a temporary lapse and had no intentions of moving out or starting a new life, etc. and from his message, I sensed that she was not all that understanding about him, even considering dating someone else.

The discussion ended with them deciding to sell their house and move their separate way. As a result of this, he was now moving house and moving on. It seemed that the split wasn't in such good terms, after all, it had only been in such good terms because she wasn't even aware it had happened!

I was pleasantly surprised, not that he recognised his error, but that he took the time to admit to it in writing. So not your usual kind of idiot. Shame I wasn't petite, with black hair, blue eyes and nowhere near a size eight.

It's complicated.

No speak no English

At times, you find some gentlemen online who live in England but come from other countries. There is nothing wrong with that. I enjoy meeting people from different cultures, languages, way of life, etc. and I feel it could give another dimension to the relationship.

Dating online would suggest that the initial contact would be written and would need to be conducted in English and, of course, this could cause a huge problem when you cannot string a sentence together.

There were times when it didn't matter how many times I re-read the message, I still didn't have a clue what it meant. This happened in my early days of online dating and I wish I had kept a few of those to quote here. Pigeon English doesn't cover it. Actually, I would have understood a pigeon much better.

Believe me, I am not talking about spelling or grammatical mistakes either. These are the forte of some very English gentlemen who clearly failed to listen and understand the most basic principles of their own language.

I do not work for the grammar police, but it is a good judge of education and potential compatibility if sentences are in such a state. Do they ever read? Even if it is only the tabloids? Write anything at work? I made the effort to learn English, why can't they?

'You wasn't' is not acceptable

'Their' belongs to someone, 'there' can be a place, 'where' is definitely a place, 'were' is what used to be, 'wear' is what you put on your in the morning and no, I don't 'of to', sorry I don't HAVE to read this rubbish!

"I thought saying hello is nice then wink," most probably translates to, "I thought saying hello would be nicer than a wink."

What would have been nicer still, if you could have expressed yourself properly, made the effort to read what you had written before sending it to ensure you didn't look illiterate.

Maybe the ones who just winked were just being wise after all!

It's complicated.

Repeat offender

I had just joined a new website in the hope that this one would have a better calibre of offers. The television advert had promised so much. I was in luck, one guy started speaking to me literally a few minutes after I uploaded my profile.

I wasn't all that surprised, I knew the drill: new blood online is always sought after. You always get the most messages in the first couple of weeks of joining. As anticipated, a message arrived. I read it and went to view the profile to see who I was talking to and noticed that said gentleman was way older than me.

Not a problem as such, but with age gaps, there is always a problem that the two of you are not in the same phase of life. If I date someone much younger than myself, he is likely to want children, to want to buy a house, etc. which I have already done. Eventually, the age gap is bound to become an issue.

Having said that, the same applies with older gentlemen. They may be retired, where I still go to work, have grandchildren and have a very different lifestyle. I didn't want to appear rude and I answered something fairly banal and close-ended so as not to encourage further messages.

The next day I received another message. I was not sure what to answer. Since some of his profile pictures were rather unusual, I thought it would give me the opportunity to enquire about them. I wondered why he had put a leaf as a profile pictures.

Of course, it wasn't a leaf. He corrected me, it was the picture of a fossil. To be honest, I hadn't seen many pictures of fossils before, whether on dating websites or elsewhere for that matter. Easy mistake to make.

I was still curious about why he thought a picture of a fossil would help him in his quest for a partner. He explained that he had put pictures of what interested him. Hence nature and animal pictures. He explained that he spent hours sitting, contemplating nature in all its aspects. I must confess, that when I think of nature, I don't automatically think fossil, but I could understand where he was coming from.

He asked me if I was contemplating nature, to which I answered that I was doing what I could to protect our planet, but would much rather spend time with others being active rather than observing nature. I also qualified my comment by saying that I have a very poor attention span, not unlike a toddler and that I was getting bored very quickly so preferred something more active. Which prompted him to say that he couldn't believe how rude I was.

This really annoyed me. I never told him he was dull; I think he jumped to that conclusion. I told him that I needed to remain active, move and that I was getting bored quickly and sitting still wasn't me at all, to be honest, I did list all my activities and hobbies on my profile, and you can easily come to the conclusion that I never sit still. That's the way I am. I wasn't going to pretend to be someone else nor desiring his approval. I was merely stating a fact. Similarly, I wasn't judging him either. I was telling him about me. That wasn't rude. The entire process of communicating online is to get to know each other and I was doing it.

I never said, "You are a boring old git." That would have been rude and that was not the answer I had given him. Live and let live is my motto. I am not here to judge. Having said that, he probably read my thoughts. Then he warned me that he wouldn't be speaking to me anymore. I wasn't distraught at the thought. Two, possibly three weeks later, I received another email from the same gentleman.

I was a little surprised to say the least, since his last message said that he would never speak to me. I enquired about his change of heart. He said he liked to give people another chance and I replied, truth be told, I did not particularly want another chance. I didn't even want the first one. I should have stopped it there and then but was in danger of becoming the rude woman he had already accused me of being.

This time he started on music. I thought it was pretty safe. He asked what I liked; I was very careful not to offend him. I mentioned that I played in an orchestra and therefore rather liked classical music but enjoyed a wide range of different genres of music. He went on, telling me about his music preferences and mainly some singers I had never heard of. I explained that I arrived in the UK in the mid '80s so prior to that my knowledge of Anglo-Saxon music is limited and artists that would have been famous in the UK may not have been known at all in where I come from.

Unfortunately, this appeared to be, once again, the wrong answer and he got very stroppy, telling me that I wasn't the woman for him and that he wasn't going to continue communicating to me. Not to harbor on a point but we had already established that fact three weeks ago. I was being rejected twice in three weeks by a guy I wasn't interested in dating in the first place. That must have been a record, I thought.

Two weeks later, another email. "I think we should meet for coffee." [*Really? How did you reach that conclusion?*] I never bothered answering, avoiding myself a third rejection.

It's complicated.

Formal

It is really difficult to answer when the first message is really formal and verging on the professional.

- - - Would you like to chat? - - -
- - - Kind regards. - - -
- - -

- - - Dear Sir, - - -
- - - no thank you. - - -
- - - Yours faithfully. - - -
- - -

It's complicated.

Too far

We had communicated online for two or three weeks and we talked about most things. I was starting to wonder whether he was one of those pen pal daters. Then one day, I had his last message: "You live too far."

I certainly hadn't moved during the time we communicated. So why even start communicating and waste my time?

It's complicated.

It's all about me, myself and I

I had exchanged a few emails with a gentleman from the other side of the county and it looked promising – good profile and from the emails I found that we had quite a lot I common.

He liked to holiday abroad, enjoyed skiing and classical

music. He quickly asked if he could ring me. I said yes and he rang almost straight after receiving my phone number.

Before I could even finish my greetings, he asked if I could ring him back because he didn't have many minutes on his contract to ring people. As I have unlimited minutes, I didn't mind but thought it was a little odd. Anyway, I rang him back.

He talked constantly for forty to forty-five minutes. First about his wife [*not another one!*], how she left him, his career change, after that his children, where he was going on a Sunday afternoon, his hobbies, his favourite classical composers, what food he enjoyed. You name it, he said it, and I knew it. I can't remember him pausing for breath. I barely said anything at all.

Then the conversation stopped as he said he had to go. I thought fair enough, thinking it wasn't a bad idea and let my ear recover. I didn't think it had gone too bad, well not as far as I was concerned since I clearly hadn't had a chance to say anything, therefore, nothing to offend or to be rude about.

I thought he was bound to want to know about me at our next encounter. The first phone call was like an introduction, he got nervous and spoke too much, now he'll want to know more about me. A few minutes later, I received a text saying, "You are not what I was expecting so will not contact you again."

Give the lady a chance! Still puzzled by that conclusion but strong by the thought that I was worth the 3p for this final text message.

Personal experience tells me that men like to talk about themselves a lot, which isn't all that attractive. Women like to feel a little special, and sitting in front of a guy just constantly talking about himself, his work, his failed marriage is not going to work.

It's complicated.

Dog owners

Profile pictures with a dog is usually a big clue that the man has a dog. As I am allergic to dog hair – quite badly allergic in fact – it is a definite NO for me. If someone with a dog on their profile picture started to converse with me I used to say, "Thanks for the message, but I noticed you have a dog and unfortunately I am allergic to your four-legged friend's hair and I feel it's too soon to ask you to choose between me or the dog!" I thought it was both polite and stating there's no hope but with a twist of humour. Usually that did the trick, except for two gentlemen who continued messaging.

One was actually a fun exchange. He started saying he could buy me space suit for when I came to visit and I suggested buying a giant hamster ball for the dog, etc. and we went on engineering all sort of devices where we could meet and me not being in contact with his dog. We never met but it was all very light-hearted and very entertaining. Good memory.

The other one carried on and wanted to meet. I said that there was little point starting a potential relationship when I knew the dog was a showstopper. We could never come to each other's place. Even if he came to mine wearing a jumper he had on when the dog was in the room with him I'd spend our time together sneezing and scratching my eyes out. To be perfectly honest, not my ideal date.

That didn't deter my admirer. Finally, I asked him what he was trying to achieve as we could never meet. He said, "Eventually, you'll come to like my dog."

Not a question of liking [*you div*], I didn't say I was allergic because I didn't like the look of your dog. It's because next to a dog, I usually have swollen eyes, runny nose, itchy throat and after a while difficulty breathing [*and I tend to like breathing more than I like dogs*], which eventually would trigger a massive asthma attack.

Once I stayed at friends with a dog and I ended up at A&E. I did explain what an allergy was, not really a question of choice or like. He stopped communicating for a couple of weeks, then sent me an email asking if I would reconsider.

Dog or breathing? Let me think that through... it's a tough one.

"Yes, I have changed my mind, this week I no longer want to breathe, it's overrated, bring on the dog!" I am not convinced he sensed the sarcasm in my answer.

It's complicated.

What's up Doc?

A doctor started to correspond with me. So far so good. On his profile, he had said he was 'separated' and as an educated man I expected him to know the true meaning of the word. We started messaging, but not too often, as we were both busy people. I enjoyed reading his messages; for once they were in English and coherent. A pleasant and welcome change.

He asked me if I appreciated he was only separated. I said yes *[I can read]* to which I added it will be OK if you are separated, pending a divorce hearing or separated as wishful thinking. He appeared to like my answer, although he never offered to clarify under which category his separation fell under.

Eventually, he asked if we could meet for coffee near his place of work. Quite honestly, I am always a bit reluctant to go far out of my way just for coffee, the travelling alone would have been in the region of £60, which would have made it an expensive cup of coffee. I offered to meet halfway and didn't get an answer.

Then another email came through from him a few days later: "I am free between 15:00 and 16:00 on Tuesday." *[Well let me drop everything to meet you, it's not as if I have a job or anything.]* I can't remember answering. After three or four days: "Are you free to meet tomorrow at 10:00am?" I couldn't recall ever having said I wasn't working. Let me take the day as annual leave on top of the cost of travelling. Each time I saw myself politely declining his persistent offer. I must say that it became a little tedious and decided to delete his number.

I didn't hear from him for a while, then out of the blue, I received a new text message: "On Saturday, I'll be in Central London in the afternoon and I am free most of the day, shall we go for coffee?"

I asked him if there was any point in getting together at all, it took us over two months to have free time together; it was not looking good and we were not going to be meeting much. His answer came soon after: "I thought we could meet have tea / coffee, or potentially a posh lunch and if we have chemistry I would invite you to my on-call room for the rest for the afternoon. But I guess it depends on how you feel about those possibilities."

Quite honestly, I didn't feel anything about 'those possibilities.' I am not after casual sex. Would I pay a subscription to a dating website, when I could go out any Friday, Saturday evening and pull someone just for a one-off? I would be saving myself a lot of time, effort and money if I was that way inclined.

It's complicated.

The fortune teller

I also came across a profile from a medium / fortune teller guy.

Not really my cup of tea but I thought worth a try. I was pondering whether he made that up to attract the ladies. I thought it may be worth checking it out. I was indeed very intrigued by his statement and asked him if he could see the future of a person without actually meeting.

Of course he could do it!

I was most impressed. He had this ability, even miles and miles away from the person who was asking. I was really keen to see how accurate his predictions could be. As I had been on this particular website for a little while, I asked if I would meet my soulmate and, more importantly, how.

Should I stay on that website for instance? The answer came as: "Yes you will meet your soulmate but not online, you are going to meet my soulmate whilst walking your dog."

Considering my dog allergy, it made me laugh out loud, a literal LOL. I never owned a dog, cannot even stay in the same room as a dog without having itchy eyes, sneezing and having an asthma attack. I do not think that is likely to happen in this life. Perhaps in another dimension, there is a version of me with a four-legged friend who enjoys taking it for long walks in the country. But not in this one.

It's complicated.

Groundhog Day

I had registered on what I finally came to consider one of the most serious dating websites. A bit more expensive, granted, but I thought that perhaps men would be a bit more interested in finding their soulmate and I bit that particular bullet. After a few days, a gentleman started emailing me. He said he used to live in the town I was living in at the time, he briefly told me about his job. The messages on the site were a bit cryptic, never too long and only had one a day, so nothing was progressing too fast.

Then he asked me out for a drink. We agreed a time and a place. The following week in a nearby pub and with this I agreed to swap mobile phone numbers. From then, I had a text in the evening saying, "Hello, how was your day today?" to which I answered and asked about his.

No reply came until the next evening when I received a new message: "Hello, how was your day?" Once again, I answered and enquired about his. Then wondered whether I should have asked about his day since I never had any answer the previous day. I thought I would end my message with another question to prompt a response. After all, he may not have wanted to discuss his day.

"Have you got any plans for this evening?" I kindly asked.

The same thing happened. No answer until the following evening.

"Hello, how was your day?"

I could hardly believe it and was starting to wonder what we were going to discuss on our date. This time my answer said, "Good day. You?"

Still no answer until the next day and once again the "Hello, how was your day?"

As it happened, that day I had run a temperature and hadn't been able to get out of bed and was dosed up on paracetamol. By that time, I had become convinced that there was no way he was reading my messages or that he was remotely interested in what I had to say. I answered nevertheless: "Not had a good day at all, stayed in bed all day with a massive cold." No further messages were received that evening.

The next evening, same time, I received the exact same text. "Hello, how was your day?"

Is there a way you can actually programme your phone to send the same text every day at the same time? You can set your Outlook to ensure emails are sent at a specific time, whether you are in front of your computer or not; perhaps that was also available on phones.

This time, I answered that I was surprised he didn't start his message by asking me if I felt better. *[Did he even read my last message?]* I didn't give him chance to assure me he had when his messages demonstrated otherwise. I was past caring and I concluded my message by saying that I no longer wished to meet him for a drink as I didn't feel we would have much to chat about.

He answered straightaway for a change: "I understand." *[Did he?]*

It's complicated.

Pen friends

During my time online, I corresponded with many men I never actually met. Some lived in a different country, which made the dating even more difficult. Not feasible.

Some days, you just need to speak to someone, and I do not even mean a real chat, but just an online chat. Because let's face it, some evenings you close your front door when you come back from work and if at first, you think great, calm and quietness… After a few hours, after a few days, weekends of complete silence, you crave human contact.

I had a few discussions from overseas. They gave you a glimpse of another life elsewhere, breaking your monotony. One of these was Danish, we discussed work and handball, one of my favourite sports. We discussed our different ways of life, etc. It was pleasant.

I also corresponded with a guy who was a keen mountain bike racer and through our conversations, we realised that we were going to the same holiday resorts, him in the summer for biking, me in the winter for skiing. Small world!

I exchanged a few messages with a beekeeper, something I knew nothing about, and a captain of a cruise liner. All had varied and interesting lives and after a few exchanges, we went our separate ways. One of my friends ended up chatting with a journalist. She admitted that without online dating she wouldn't have had the opportunity to meet a journalist.

These unusual brief encounters were nice. Opening your horizons a little, not to mention an enjoyable way to spend a couple of hours on an evening when nothing else is available. The conversation never led to a meeting, but that was almost a given considering the geography. What I couldn't understand is people who write to you via the dating site and who live spitting distance from you, tell you everything about their life and still never offer to meet.

One of them was actually local, in the village next to where I live and never ever asked me out for a drink in the couple of months he corresponded with me. Surely it would have been so much easier to meet up for a drink.

Those were irritating because it became apparent after a few messages that you had very little in common and that the conversation led absolutely nowhere and was in no way entertaining.

I finally came to the conclusion that many guys who send you emails have actually no intention of meeting you.

They messaged you most days, telling you about their day, work, the traffic on the way to work, what they have for tea, their plans for the weekend and yet after weeks of messages, there has never been an attempt to meet.

They just want a pen pal. Some will even push the twist into facetiming for hours with you from a room when their partner was still in the bedroom next door.

It's complicated.

On your way to a date

Now that you have messaged a few times and started to get a little more acquainted, you agree to exchange email addresses and wish to make it a little friendlier. Having said that, I created a new email address for the purposes of online dating. One that wouldn't reveal my full name. You can never be too careful. If your newly found friend is as genuine as the profile describes, then you'll soon meet and it won't matter, but until then it is still best to remain cautious.

So, you have agreed to meet, exchanged email addresses, even phone numbers. You exchanged phone numbers and then what? Do you ring or text? Or wait for him to do the first move? Whatever you decide, common sense will dictate not to do drunk texting send the wrong text, intentionally or not. Text something that makes sense, if you want an answer. Don't over text.

By all means, remain consistent with what you previously said online, on email or a previous text or it makes it really easy to realise you are talking to different people about the same thing. Don't tell your mate you are on a date and add a few chosen details and send it to you by mistake. It doesn't look all that good.

Above all, txtin lk ths is no longr Kool, besides we have all passed the age of Nokia phones and 'I *no how busy u r*' or '*u where tired*' just winds me up.

It's complicated.

4

. . .

DATING

It's all good, you have gone through the profile, exchanged a few emails, sometimes even spoken on the phone, and you decide to meet.

You follow the rules: always meet in a public place. You agonise over what to wear, hair, makeup, shoes, etc. look at their profile again to check – of course you make an effort, you are going out, it's the first meeting, so you would like to make a good impression. Not dissimilar to an interview, the first impression counts, or so you are lead to believe because when you arrive there, you could be confronted with the down and out look or one of Colin Firth's jumpers in Bridget Jones. Because naturally, you should be privileged that someone gave you the time of day!

Well not all of them, but most don't even think. It doesn't matter what they wear; they consider themselves irresistible so why should they think they need to make an effort?

DO

- ✿ Let friends, or perhaps family members, know where you're going and when you'll be home;
- ✿ Meet in a public place with lots of people around;
- ✿ Use your own transportation to get to and from the date;
- ✿ Watch your alcohol intake; you don't want to make yourself vulnerable or be remembered for the wrong reasons;
- ✿ Keep your purse, wallet, phone and personal items with you;
- ✿ Leave at any time if you feel uncomfortable;
- ✿ Bring your mobile phone with you; and
- ✿ Arrange to contact a friend when the date is over.

DON'T

- ✿ Go on your date without telling anyone;
- ✿ Meet somewhere isolated or at your or someone else's home;
- ✿ Allow your date to pick you up at your home, hotel or place of work;
- ✿ Leave your drink unattended;
- ✿ Leave your personal items unattended;
- ✿ Feel pressured to stay or do anything; and
- ✿ Go to a place where you can't contact anyone.

And never worry or feel embarrassed about your behaviour if you want to end a date. Your safety comes first. It is far more important than the other person's opinion of you.

To call or not to call before the first meeting? You still haven't decided.

Topics of conversation during the date: avoid politics and religion like anything else. You still want to find out more about that person, so a few questions are OK, but it's not the Spanish Inquisition.

Anyway, you have made a decision. Told your friends you were going and where you are going. You don't want to be late and scatty and not too early and appearing desperate. You know where you are going, you look good and off you go to meet your potential match.

Don't look too good, you could still meet Mr White Socks in Sandals, remember. It is best to remain casual and yet not too casual that you look as if you haven't made an effort. First impressions do matter.

It's complicated.

FIRST DATES

Currently extremely topical; they have even made a TV series about it. It is already a sensitive subject when there are just the two people on your first date. I can't bear imagining what it must be like when the entire nation is watching.

Stingy or what?

Who should pay for the first date?

Once again, I logged on, read a profile. A few emails later, we decided to meet one evening. Since he mentioned that he thought going for a meal for a date could be costly, I suggested going to a local pizza place – not generally expensive and I happened to have a voucher. The meal was as expected. The conversation and company were bordering on the lower side of average. Really nothing to write home about, although the ex-girlfriend came up a lot. Work and children also came up; nothing out of the ordinary.

At the end of the meal, I got my vouchers out, left them on the table and went to the ladies. When I came back to the table, he was analysing the bill. He complained that the voucher wasn't a huge discount after all and took £15 out of his wallet, then asked me for £15, saying that it should include a big enough tip.

Unfortunately, his generosity hadn't stretched to paying my share of the bill. He left, promising to soon be in touch but never contacted me again. To tell the truth, I was quite happy with that decision. Having said that, at least he paid his share.

On a few occasions, I did encounter that classic: "Sorry, I forgot my wallet, do you mind?" Some even offered to pay at a later point, when they knew so well there wouldn't be a second date. Should there be a second meeting, you are cautious and avoid the offer of another meal for obvious reasons.

The cherry on top of that particular cake came when not only did he not have his wallet to pay for the date but also had not enough petrol in his car to go home and asked if you could go to the nearest petrol station with him and buy him some fuel. I didn't want to appear stingy but was also wondering what type of fool I had been on a date with. There is a fine line and that was going way over it!

Another similar situation had happened a few years prior with Dartford Bridge toll in the days when you still had to pay at the toll booth. I was first contacted by a 'thanks for the wink' which encouraged me to look at the profile despite the fact that I was pretty certain I hadn't winked. For one, I rarely winked at men and looking at his profile, we definitely had nothing in common. It was the early days of my dating experience and thought I wouldn't judge a book by its cover, aka, not judge anyone by the profile.

I made the decision to carry on chatting online for a bit and we agreed to meet for coffee in a shopping centre more or less halfway but it meant that he would have to cross the Thames. The conversation didn't really flow and took a weird turn when he mentioned taking his ex to court; she was a psycho. etc. and he wasn't dropping it.

Then the restraining order came up; I thought it was a little concerning, but roll with it. After all, the first date is a fact-finding experience. All very good to know that the Ex was a bad person and lucky for me, he was OK.

Following that natter, I knew that coffee was going to be just coffee and not cake and was keen to make a swift escape without arranging another date.

The bill arrived and we had two coffees so he read the bill and advised me how much my latte was. This statement was followed by: "And if you could give me 50p for the bridge as I had to pay for the Dartford crossing to come and see you." I thought it was a joke. He was not joking. Deadly serious in fact. So I gave him the money for my latte and a 50p coin.

We left the place and as I was on my way back to my car, he followed me and said, "Can we hold hands?" *[Err NO.]* Quickly followed by: "When can we meet again?" Well, considering how special you have made me feel in the past forty minutes… never!

It's complicated.

Schoolgirl error

I went for a drink once, possibly one of my dullest dates.

As the conversation progressed he mentioned about his youngest daughter and where she was at school. Both my girls were at the same school, I decided that would be the end of that.

Far too close for comfort.

It's complicated.

Not on your turf

Where to meet is always an interesting choice. For obvious safety reasons it needs to be in a public place, coffee shop, restaurant, etc. but try to avoid going to the same pub or restaurant for your first dates or you could get a reputation not to be proud of.

Once, we had agreed to meet for a drink after work and, since he was local to me, we had agreed to go to a pub I usually go with my friends. We usually choose that pub as it is friendly and very quiet and you can hear each other and have a decent chat without having to shout. I thought it would be ideal for a first date where you are trying to get to know someone.

Wrong!

We went there and it was indeed quiet. Unfortunately, unbeknown to me some of my friends were in the room next door. I hadn't seen them, but they saw me.

The following week, I went to choir rehearsals as normal, and the people who had seen me started their twenty questions: "Who was the tall guy I saw you with? Where did you meet him? What does he do?"

This went on for a bit and was extremely difficult, because although we had had a very nice evening and we did get on; had a similar sense of humour but he wasn't boyfriend material, nor was I his choice either, but we did meet again afterward as friends.

Indeed, it is good to follow the advice to go to a public place you know well, only not that well.

It's complicated.

ALMOST A FIRST DATE

At times, organising a single date seems to be the most difficult venture.

Yes, my lord, I'll drop everything for you!
On a couple of occasions, I went through weeks of written communication via email or text – not that there was anything wrong with that, before organising that all-important first date. It was, however, a lot of effort for not much result.

The first one was a sales representative. He was travelling around the country quite a bit. I understood from his correspondence that most of his messages were actually sent to me whilst he was on the other side of the country. Then he said, "I am coming home this weekend, perhaps we should meet."

I agreed. As it happened, I had very little organised for that particular weekend and I asked, "Which day this weekend would you prefer?"

"I can't this weekend, I am seeing my kids."

"OK." *[Why offer to meet this weekend if you are not available?]*

The following week, he went on his travels and assured me 'when I am back next weekend, we can meet'. This time it was my turn to see my daughters and kindly declined the offer. His answer came almost immediately: "Do you want to meet or not?"

"Yes of course *[although the tone almost prompted me to say, not actually that bothered]* but I have made prior plans with my daughters, perhaps we can organise something during the week."

"I am working during the week."

"Aren't we all?"

"OK, let's try to organise something for next Thursday, I am coming back from work and it's a nice round trip on the M25 and I may not be early. So, let's say late Thursday," he suggested.

"Thursday, it is. Let's say after 20:30, it should give you time to come back from your lap of the M25 and will allow me to go to choir, which finishes at 20:30. Perfect."

Never heard from him again. I assumed I said the wrong thing, but still unsure what it was.

It's complicated.

The second man messaged me for months, at least three months' worth of messages. I thought he would fall in the 'I want a pen pal' category. Only in the beginning, there were lots of messages stating that we should meet. I hadn't disagreed. We tried to arrange a meeting halfway between the two of us. It was all going back and forth and suddenly no answer to my messages. I was wondering what had happened to him. I asked if he was OK.

Still no answer.

I left it at that, to be honest there wasn't as a lot I could do. He clearly didn't want to talk anymore and I didn't insist. About six weeks later, a new message: "Hello there. Remember me? How are you?"

A bit random, but despite my surprise, I replied, "I am fine thanks, what happened to you?"

He went on explaining that he had 'stuff' to resolve before starting something new, which I thought was highly commendable. I wished more people were like him. We started almost where we left off. I asked if the 'stuff' was actually resolved and he said yes. I thought we were all good to go. How wrong can you be?

After a few days of 'how's your day going?' We decided to arrange a date. Once again, I tried to arrange something halfway. He said he didn't mind coming to me as he didn't know the town and perhaps I could show him the highlights. With this answer, we arranged to meet for lunch the following Sunday.

Unfortunately, he had to cancel on Friday as he had to go and see his brother who told him that apparently his house had been broken into and he needed to go and have a look.

I wasn't sure why the brother got involved as he didn't live near the house and wondered why if you lived 200 miles away from your old house you would not leave your keys with a friend or neighbour living nearby for them to have a look. It seems like a sensible thing to do. But what do I know? I live on my own and only have one house.

And so, he went. On a Monday morning, I had a rundown of what had happened and he thanked me for being understanding about the short notice cancellation. Our first meeting was put back to the following weekend, Saturday night, for a meal in my town. He explained that he didn't mind driving and wanted to make up for the previous weekend.

The Friday came and messaged that he was still 'shaken up' by the break-in which had been committed by his ex-girlfriend and he believed he would need to get to court and get an injunction against her and perhaps he should be doing that at the weekend.

I knew where this was leading to. Although I didn't think that the injunction and our date on the evening were mutually exclusive. One could have easily taken place during the day the other in the evening. Cynical me could see a pattern developing and I said, "Not a problem, do everything you feel you have to do."

I was pretty reasonable about it, if I may say so myself. To tell the truth, I thought that it was Friday and a friend had asked me out and his decision was leaving me free to go out with her which sounded a much more entertaining evening.

Same thing on Monday, full of thanks for my understanding for the short notice. I had plans for the following weekend so no meetings were organised which turned out to be a godsend as he had to go to court and spend another weekend at his old house to put it on the market. The next attempt at seeing each other ended up with yet another last-minute cancellation for reason of 'not feeling well'.

I suppose these things happen. I had virtually given up on the date, then one Thursday, I received a text: "What are you doing this weekend? Shall we meet on Sunday?"

"I am seeing my friend in the evening at 5:00ish but free before that." And with that offer, I was thinking, "Lunch date maybe?"

No answer came.

Complete silence. The entire Friday, Saturday, nothing.

On a Sunday morning, I broke the silence and asked whether we were meeting later on or not. Sadly, this prompted a long text of abuse, saying that I was rude, disorganised, had no respect for anyone. That he was really pleased that we hadn't met, that I was selfish, too engrossed in myself and it went on and on.

I wasn't quite sure what to say really and answered that I was really sorry he felt that way. I thought I had been very patient with him whilst he was sorting his 'stuff' – his injunction, his house – and I wasn't going to cancel my friend at short notice, unlike him, especially when there was still ample time for the two of us to meet on Sunday.

Evidently, he had enough people like me. Maybe he referred to his previous girlfriend and couldn't help but feel a likeness between her and me.

It's complicated.

Night shift workers

All very well and good; as usual, a new gentleman contacts you, possibly winks and you start chatting. Sometimes, you even develop a good banter. You have a similar sense of humour, it is all going well. In some cases, it seems that you have a lot in common, one was actually a fan of foreign films, mainly European which was quite unusual, only his choice of film directors left a lot to be desired.

We talked for a while, exchanged phone numbers, sent texts then the conversation moved to 'what do you do for a living?' and then they tell you: 'I work nights in a factory or that they are an HGV driver and travel at night only'. Not that there is anything wrong with these professions, I just don't believe they are conducive to starting new relationships. Having such different timetables can't make things easy.

It is also easy to understand why they have had a string of relationships that didn't survive, where the wives and girlfriends were not being as faithful during those nights as the marriage vows had promised. Basically, what they are offering is to be with you and yet spend five evenings and five nights out of seven on your own. Of course, in a moment of madness, you think, well why not if he is the one? And then you start planning a date.

Well, not that easy... because at the end of the day, when you come back from work they are going to work and at the weekend – well Friday night – they are still working so nothing till Saturday afternoon. This leaves you the entire Saturday afternoon and evening to do something together, and possibly the Sunday during the day if nothing else gets in the way.

As I found out Sunday evening, they tend to go to bed very late to start getting ready for the night shifts of the week ahead, but for you, Sunday night is a school night. After all, I am not that keen to stay up too late and start the week exhausted, work does that for you, you don't really need someone adding to it.

So basically, they have only one night in the week free to do anything; this is Saturday night and then, of course, the rest of the time your communications channels are limited to an early morning text and then mid-afternoon communication.

Seems like a recipe for the perfect relationship, if you don't communicate, you are saved the arguments! Funnily enough, the ones I have met like that have had many failed marriages and relationships – one of them admitted to me that all the men on his shift were all single.

The only one in a happy relationship was with a woman who also worked in the same place also doing the same night shifts as her partner. I am not sure I was prepared to change career path.

It's complicated.

Headache

You receive a text while getting ready for a date forty-five minutes before your date:

"What are you doing?"

"Getting ready."

"What for?" [*What for? I thought we had a date.*]

"Are we not meeting later on?"

"I have a bit of a headache."

"?" [*So men also get headaches?*]

"I may lie down for a bit."

"Are you cancelling this evening then?"

"Not cancelling, postponing."

"To when?"

"Not sure."

That or nothing

I had been for coffee with a guy who thought we had a lot in common. It was always interesting to see what we did actually have in common. Generally, it was never a lot.

The websites suggest it is a good way to start the conversation, for the nervous newcomer to online dating. What they forget to mention is that it only works when you do have something in common. Otherwise, it makes you look like a fool.

In that very case, we had one thing in common, which was skiing. Although he admitted to being a boarder, I let him off as it is still pretty similar. Besides that, our lives were pretty dissimilar but it didn't have to mean not compatible. When I asked about his next trip to the snow, he didn't have any plans, and about his last one, it was a number of years ago. It was just coffee and it was a pleasant enough hour.

We decided to part on our different ways for that day and agreed to meet again soon. We carried on texting for a week or so and the following weekend he asked, "Shall we go to Frankie & Benny's on Tuesday?"

"Sorry, I can't do Tuesday. Can you do another day of the week?"

I never heard from him again. That was the end of that. My one and only chance and I missed it!

It's complicated.

Not THAT desperate! Thanks

Another day, another contact. Once again, profile and pictures appeared to be normal and the messages were decent enough. I answered and we started to converse.

After a few days, he asked me out on a date: "I think we should meet soon," and I agreed. As he lived a good few miles away, I suggested that we met halfway.

"I can't drive so you'll have to come to me," was his answer.

"Fair enough."

Although I wasn't quite sure what to make of the 'can't drive'.

In our day and age, I must say it was rather unusual. I didn't want to ask the reason why, as I thought there would be plenty of opportunities to ask during our date. Although I must say that first date on your turf can end up embarrassing, but I thought that if that's what he wants let's go for it and it will give me the opportunity to venture a little further than usual.

I look online where the place was, TomTom reckoned forty-five / fifty minutes. It was all acceptable and I started to look at restaurants in town to look for a suitable venue for our first date. There was quite a big choice of places and I enquired to see if there was a restaurant he could recommend. The response came almost instantaneously: "We are not eating, it's just coffee." That answer left me feeling all special.

"Let's leave it then." I am not driving for almost two hours for a coffee.

It's complicated.

KMN (Kill Me Now)

Following the usual pattern, I had been contacted by a new man. He had made a little pun about my profile, proving that he had read it, which prompted me to respond and look at his profile. Nothing too remarkable about the profile, it all appeared normal.

We had the usual 'get to know each other' messaging and I remember him being concerned about me going skiing. I thought it weird to be so concerned about my skiing in the first few messages. He explained that he had never skiied and wasn't prepared to try. I found it a little narrow-minded not knowing about a sport and yet being dead set on not even giving it a go. He went on, saying that because of the skiing he was not sure that we were suited.

Again, still a bit of an odd thing to state since it was on my profile from the onset. One of my pictures is of me in the snow, with skis, helmet, etc. He couldn't have missed them when he first contacted me. I answered nevertheless that it may not be an activity he would like to share with me and I could understand but went on, explaining that living in the UK, with the British landscape not being one of the high white peaks, the actual skiing part was, by default, not something you did every weekend. At the most, it was going to be two weeks out of fifty-two and that would be in a good year.

He generously conceded that he would let me go skiing for one week as long as I let him go away for a week with his football friends. Not a huge deal to agree to, so I accepted the compromise and we decided to meet face to face.

The first date took place in a local restaurant. The food was nice. Unfortunately, the conversation ran dry a few times but new surroundings, nerves, etc. could have been the cause. It is always difficult to predict how an evening is going to pan out. After the meal, we went our separate ways. I thanked him for a nice evening, as it was. Not a rib-cracking type of evening, but it was pleasant enough.

We met again for coffee and cake and another meal. The dialogue was always a bit slow. I suppose some people are more comfortable with silence than others. By now, I was started to wonder if we ever were going to have a laugh or anything worth conversing about. Still thinking it could be nerves, he had alleged he had been single for a while after all and didn't want to appear a bit of a man-eater and thought I'd give him time to blossom.

He said that if I was free the following Saturday he'd cook for me. I said I wasn't free the entire evening as I had to go to the theatre at some point but accepted the offer of home-cooked food to be shared.

Saturday arrived, I went to his place as agreed. The house was dark and lifeless, little decoration, little at all, very bleak in fact. We sat down for dinner. Overcooked meat with overcooked frozen peas and frozen carrots. Which was OK. Since I hadn't cooked myself I couldn't really complain, but I must confess I was expecting something a little more elaborate.

We had dinner in silence. I remember thinking that should he wish to enter a religious order where you make a vow of silence he would be ready for it. Nothing much else to report. We ate dinner and did not have much time before having to leave for my drama rehearsal. With hindsight, it was a welcome excuse to move on with my evening.

We went to the lounge and sat on the sofa. He proudly stated, "I bought this a while ago in the DFS sale." I wasn't quite sure what possible witty remark I could make from that and went with: "Very nice, very comfortable."

Looking at the bare walls, he hazarded an: 'I am in the middle of decorating' in case I hadn't noticed. The curtains were down with no pictures on the wall, not that there were many in the decorated rooms either; the toolbox was on the floor, the paints brushes and pots were scattered in the middle of the lounge.

I felt the need to ask. "What colour have you gone for?"

"Dark brown," showing me the pot of paint, "to match the virtually black leather sofa and dark brown carpet. My son helped me choose the colour."

"I see," was my answer, not wanting to show too much of my opinions.

I was hardly going to volunteer my real thoughts: "Good choice! This will make a dark and dull house even darker." I refrained. Sometimes I know how to. It was getting painful and I said, "Oh dear, is that the time? I need to go." And I went. It was becoming apparent that, skiing or not, we were definitely not suited.

I hadn't quite built up the courage to say that it wasn't going to go very far and I continued answering his messages that week. Messages advising me that the radiators were being removed to paint behind, radiators being put back on, a little leak to be repaired, first coat being applied, busy at work the rest of the week so won't be able to finish painting, left work early to be able to paint. Reading his emails, I felt I was literally watching the paint dry.

He offered not to see each other at the weekend so that he could really crack on and finish the painting. Definitely a very good plan! He asked me for tea again and I said yes and went with the full intention to say face to face that he was very nice guy but not for me. I added that on that particular evening I wouldn't be able to stay long as I was trying to give myself a get out clause, just in case.

We had the exact same dinner as the previous time. He probably had to finish the bag of frozen peas. This is the problem with being too polite the first time and saying it was nice, you risk being served the same thing again.

I went home and thought: "Right be brave and tell him you can't see a future," and I did. It was remarkably difficult, he hadn't done anything wrong or untowards. I was starting to wonder whether his ex had died of boredom.

I was brave and told him something to that effect, 'it's not you, it's me', when in fact it clearly was him but thought that it was best to blame myself here. Unfortunately, he didn't take it very nicely and told me that in fact, I wasn't right for him as I was clearly unwilling to dedicate him enough of my time.

It's complicated.

Don't want to date

One of my friend's sisters had just married someone she met on a website I had never heard of. Could there be a better testimony than a real one? As a result, I decided to give that website a try. Nothing ventured... as they say.

I certainly was hopeful. To tell the truth, the database was small, but the profiles were a little more elaborate. Could it mean that the potential candidates were somewhat nicer? More genuine too? Maybe it will work for me too? As it happened there wasn't much affinity with anyone online at that particular time but it provided me half-decent banter and coffee dates.

Within a few days on that site, I had a date organised for the following weekend. I was looking forward to that date, much more than the others. Mainly because the conversations we exchanged leading up to that date were truly enjoyable. We did have a lot in common. I just liked the sound of that date.

The weekend arrived and we went for a coffee and ended up having a few more and stayed chatting for a while. As we left, he revealed he had a great time and asked if I would like to go on another date. Did I? Is the Pope Catholic? I thought we got on fabulously. We talked, laughed, shared quite a few interests. He was nicely spoken, pleasant and rather good-looking. One of my better starts, I thought.

"Yes," I eagerly replied.

He asked once more, "Are you sure?

I was.

He continued by saying that he would contact me shortly with a date and place.

It was all good and I was looking forward to a second meeting. We exchanged a few texts and emails for the next couple of days and then nothing. I didn't want to appear too clingy or needy so I left it for a couple of days or so. After all, we all have a life to live. The following weekend arrived and I was rather disappointed that he hadn't made any offer in respect of the second date since he seemed so keen the previous week.

I bit the bullet and asked him, "So, do tell when were you thinking of having this second date?" His answer came almost immediately: "I am not sure I want to date again." Disappointed, didn't even cover it. I nevertheless wished him good luck for the future.

Not wanting to date? Why bother with a dating website? Isn't that a massive waste of both money, time, but, more importantly, waste of MY TIME?

It's complicated.

Doing it?

I had been feeling very smug when I was contacted by this new man. He was very cute and I thought that I was potentially punching above my weight, but he contacted and I didn't want to be rude so I answered.

After a few days of exchanging messages, we decided to meet for a drink. Then went for another one as the first one had gone very well.

For one reason or another, we hadn't been able to arrange a third date but we were still in contact. Then out of the blue, I receive a text message: "When are we doing it?" I first thought it would be in respect of another date but stood to be corrected: doing it was doing it!

I was obviously dealing with a true romantic. I supposed we were on a dating site and we had been on two (short) dates, but still not quite what I was after.

It's complicated.

5

MORE THAN ONE SUCCESSFUL DATE

COULD HE BE THE ONE?

Black & White

As I was looking at my daily matches, I was also surfing the internet for potential ski resorts for the forthcoming season. The computer system had matched me with a guy who lived nearby. He had given his name as Max, although that turned out to be incorrect. I am not sure I can see the point of giving a false name as you are displaying a picture of yourself. It seems a bit pointless to me. He had also lied about his age by one year – that should have raised alarm bells – but the best is still to come.

Anyway, the picture was nice and profile looked normal. He was a skiier, a bonus as far as I was concerned. I stopped my internet search for a moment to ask him if he had a favourite resort and perhaps provide some inspiration as to where to book for the winter. He answered straight away, stating that he owned a chalet in the Swiss Alps and that he always went there to ski.

I was suitably impressed, I therefore answered, "Forget the dating, if you ever need a skiing partner I am your man, so to speak." Next message was his phone number.

We met a few times, talked about our lives. We got on well, everything appeared to be going smoothly and we agreed to go skiing together in his chalet. I thought he was a bit cagey whilst discussing his situation vis a vis seeing his sons. He had also said, "It's complicated," when referring to his family life. I should have known better and yet gave the benefit of the doubt. There could still be a sensitive, honest man out there. It could have been a bad split with wife, she could make it difficult and it could be recent hence painful. Cynical Me thought, "You still live with them and their mother and the awkwardness only comes because you are not divorced." I shared my views with some of my friends and family and opinions were divided. I couldn't tell for sure.

Anyway, we continued seeing each other for a couple of weeks and planned our week skiing. He booked the flights and the lift passes, and we were on our way. I couldn't wait.

When we got there, the chalet was amazing, spacious and warm. Situated on a hill, it gave every room its own breathtaking view. It was picturesque and nicely decorated. After unpacking in the chalet's master bedroom. I felt rather sick. I blamed it on the plane catering and I was rather hoping it wouldn't last long as I was keen to go for my first ski of the season. I was making my way to the kitchen for some water when he said to me, "You'll need to make yourself scarce as I need to ring home."

Ta-dah!

Of course, he was still living with his wife and sons and had told them he was going to the chalet to sort bits of DIY, see renting agents, etc. No mention of me and even less of his online dating. I was not even surprised! I told him that I was not going to be part of that deal. I would be quite happy to finish the skiing holiday as friends and was going to move my stuff into another bedroom. He didn't take to my reaction too nicely and was quickly told that 'other women' *[Other women? I wasn't even the first one! He was using his chalet as a bachelor's pad well away from his wife and sons. Unbelievable!]* had been privileged to be invited to the chalet and had enjoyed a very good time! He wasn't talking about the skiing either, more of the après ski, because none of the others, from what I understood, could actually ski.

Unfortunately for him, the après ski had suddenly slid out of reach and then skiing would be the only purpose of the holiday, as I don't do sleeping with married men. The atmosphere became a little frosty. But it was a skiing holiday, after all!

He assured me that I wouldn't regret the après ski. *[Of course not!]*

Did he honestly think that with that, kind of comment I would change my mind and jump in bed with him? Yes, he did! Anyway, I would not regret sticking to my principles either.

Then he explained to me that in fact, I wouldn't have to breach my principles as he actually never married the mother of his sons. Therefore, he was not a married man and stated that he had been on dating sites for years, some had even specialising in married people.

That, I didn't know. You do learn something every day. Some days, the newly acquired knowledge isn't going to enhance your life at all. It was one of those days for me. I must be too old fashioned and boring for the twenty-first century. Am I the only one still believing in monogamy? Being faithful and loyal to the man you love? In his views, not having declared his marriage vows to promise to be faithful to the mother of his sons gave him a licensce to pursue his continuous search for new sexual partners.

I was told that I was the one with the 'problem' and I was far too black and white for this day and age. Unquestionably, I was the one with a problem!

It's complicated.

Liar, liar, pants on fire

The online dating world is vastly populated by married men. Maybe it's just me attracting that type of person. Some are quite openly still married, searching for a bit on the side. Some are 'separated', generally in their heads more than anything else, and my first encounter of that kind was in my early days of online dating. This particular gentleman was living nearby, so quite handy to meet for coffee or to share a meal, which I was grateful for. If anything, it also offered companionship on a few evenings.

He had also said 'it's complicated' when he related his situation with his children and ex-wife. They were living in another part of the country. He lived nearby Monday to Friday for work then went to his other house in the home counties at the weekend to see his young children. I was suitably impressed with his commitment to seeing his family. Running two houses and going there dutifully every weekend.

The dating was going well. It was contained to weekdays as his weekends were spent elsewhere. After a few weeks, things started to trouble me. He had invited me over for tea one evening and whispered as he was reaching for something in the top cupboard, "Oh I really hurt myself this weekend."

"Doing what? I asked concerned.

"DIY, my ex needed some bits done."

I must admit I was surprised. "You do DIY for your ex at the weekend?"

"Well yes, she is the mother of my children."

So she was and from all accounts, she was also the one who had an affair and ruined the marriage. He had told me the story with such emotion, the tears were still streaming down his cheeks. I believed him. Interesting to know that when she decided he was no longer good enough for her, he was still her 'chosen' one for the DIY. He had clearly forgiven, but not forgotten, the affair and the breakdown of the marriage. I found that a little weird but you can't really come back to 'the mother of my children' and decided to drop it.

A few weeks later, on a Sunday evening, he came back earlier than usual from his weekend away. We had agreed that I would cook a meal for the two of us. I prepared the food. He arrived as anticipated and said, "I am not too hungry because my ex cooked a massive lunch." Still fairly amazed by that comment: "You had lunch with your ex?"

"Yes, we are not at each other's throats you know, I can have lunch with her when I want to and she is the mother of my children."

It was good to be reminded, in case I had forgotten the discussion of the previous weekend.

I have what I would call a good relationship with my ex-husband. We have been divorced for many years and now I quite enjoy going with him to our daughters' events like the degree ceremonies, weddings, etc.... We end up having an enjoyable day each time. But we never do lunch, never have done, nor do I know many people having lunch with their ex either. I don't believe this is uncommon. He certainly never comes running to help with my DIY and I am also the mother of his daughters. Different people act in different ways, I suppose. I didn't want to appear like some psychotic girlfriend so thought this situation was definitely unusual, but hey, live and let live.

One day, I can't remember how the conversation started, but I asked what his ex did for a living. "Nothing," he answered. "I support her and my children 100%." The accountant in me reacted quite quickly. He had proudly said to me once how much he earned, which was the very same amount as me. Now, he was telling me that on that salary, he could afford a flat in town, a three-bed house for him to visit his children, another house for your ex-wife and family and that he supported all three of them and himself.

I was impressed because I certainly couldn't stretch my monthly income that far.

Unless...

I won the lottery,

I came from a wealthy family,

Or, if I only had one house in the home counties and assuming that the house where my 'ex' and children lived and the house I visited every weekend to see my son and daughter was one and the same. I didn't want to judge too quickly but was starting to smell a rat here.

I thought I would play Sherlock for a few days and get to the bottom of it.

Towards the end of that week, as he was going back to his other house I suggested, "I may book the cinema or something for next week; I'll give you a ring at the weekend to organise."

"I'll ring you, I have lots on this weekend," came his answer.

"OK." and I left it at that. He dutifully rang, sounding slightly out of breath.

"I wasn't expecting a heavy breathing type of phone call," I said jokingly. "What on earth are you up to?"

"Just walking the dog, thought I would ring you now."

Me, thrilled at the multitasking attempt: "I see. How's your weekend going?" and the conversation continued for the rest of the walk.

"Sorry, I never looked at the cinema, will call you tomorrow," he promised.

It is a little more complex to look at the cinema when you're walking a dog!

Sunday came and he apologised for not having a chance to ring for very long; it was just a quick phone call during the morning dog's walk. I was starting to feel seriously special by these dog-walking calls. Are there no other times to ring? [*possibly not if he wanted to be out of earshot.*]

Thinking back, I had never noticed, but all his phone calls at weekends had been during the dog's walk! No better time the entire weekend to have a chat!! By that time, I was becoming more and more suspicious.

Operation Sherlock resumed over the following week by casually enquiring: "Do you think we could spend a weekend together at some point?"

"Of course." But no offer of when or where or what would you like to do, etc.

"It would be nice to spend a whole day together as opposed to a few hours after work on a weekday," I tentatively enquired.

"Yes."

"Do you see your kids every weekend, when you go down there?" I inquired.

"No, not every weekend, every other weekend," he answered.

"That's usually the drill." I added, "Are you seeing them next week or was your weekend last week?"

"Last week," was his definite answer. [*Interesting.*]

On the one hand, that could explain why our telephone natters were made whilst walking the dog, maybe to avoid questions from children. On the other hand, he had left them unattended, home alone at least twice during the weekend. Going all that way to see them and going to walk the dog on your own is not all that wise.

"Perhaps next weekend we could do something together? What do you think?" I tentatively enquired.

Him, with the face of fear: "NO, not next weekend!"

"Do you have any plans?" I asked innocently.

"Bits and pieces in the house."

"Cool, I could go with you and help, I find DIY therapeutic."

He started to look increasingly worried and added, "No you can't go, my children will be there!"

"I thought you said they were there last week. It would be nice to see your weekend home. It would be like a weekend breakaway in the country for me."

"You can't meet my children, it's too soon."

"I agree, much too soon, but this is not what I was suggesting, besides, this weekend they will be with their mum, so it'll be fine."

He was getting angrier by the second and reacted as if I had keyed his car, started to use his credit cards and sold his worldly possession on eBay.

"There is NO WAY you are coming with me and that's that!" he splattered out.

"OK then, if it is too close to home for comfort, let's go somewhere else."

Sadly, we never went away at the weekend, or any other for that matter. I was far too ridiculous, irrational and had serious problems, mainly with trusting people. Listening to him, I was borderline psychotic. I had clearly touched a nerve, that's for sure.

And he went on and on. I dared suggest that perhaps he was hiding something and there could be a reason he got so uptight with my simple request to spend a weekend with him.

I hadn't appreciated how unreasonable that was. I was getting increasingly convinced that perhaps he wasn't as divorced as he had led me to believe and that he was leading a double life. Of course, I was wrong to even suggest it and he told me no relationship could last if there was not any trust.

He was correct on this; I never trusted him to be divorced at all and left.

It's complicated.

What's wrong with me? Oh yes, I am rude!

One summer – in August, to be precise – the system had matched me with a new potential. To this day, I still couldn't see how we were a match, possibly as a result of both being registered on a very small database and living in the same country.

We starting messaging online first, then on the phone. The usual, with the exception that this time the conversation was truly flowing. We actually got on really well, we had the same sense of humour and could talk for hours and hours, really having a nice time.

We finally met at the end of September. The first actual date went swimmingly well. We had a lovely meal in a halfway house pub. Great time! He was the perfect gentleman, taking me back to my car and waiting for me to leave before going back to his car. I was impressed. We went for dinner, cinemas, etc. and always ended up having a fantastic time together.

After a couple of months, I invited him over for dinner one evening. I got a bottle of wine out, offered him a glass and he declined, saying that he was driving later. I didn't insist, becoming more and more impressed by his self-control and good manners. He was clearly not after one thing, which I really like. We talked on the phone most days rather than messaging. We played games on the phone, like listening to little bits of music and guessing the name of the songs, artists, etc.... that sort of innocent, sweet thing, discovering each other in a way.

And so continued the platonic dating.

I invited him for a few meals and again he didn't stay. Eventually, he accepted the offer of wine and stayed at home for the night and, to my surprise, continued to demonstrate the same level of self-control even when sharing the same bed. As we were approaching the end of November by then, I thought that a kiss, possibly a cuddle wouldn't be superfluous and was starting to drop hints to that effect, which didn't produce any reaction.

I went away for a couple of weeks in early December and we didn't see each other for two weeks. During the holiday, he rang me asking when I would be back home as he was missing our little chats. I felt really chuffed about that, I thought that it was a bit of a slow start, but he likes me! Things were certainly looking up. I came back from my holidays and he came over the very next day. Same scenario as before. I was wondering what was wrong with me. There is a fine line between being shy and not interested. I had to tackle the issue and raised it during one of our many evening phone calls.

I was reassured that nothing was wrong, just he never jumped into anything too quickly. [*Well, you don't say!*] Anyway, after more phone conversations and yet more laughter, we decided that he should come and spend the following weekend at my home, more than five months into this unusual relationship. I thought the time was right; we knew each other better by then and it didn't appear to be such a big leap.

He arrived Saturday afternoon, a bit later than anticipated, but that was OK, after all, he still had bits to do in his place before coming over. We chatted. I cooked dinner and he commented that he wasn't a great fan of what I was preparing. I was a little upset considering I had asked him what he fancied and made a suggestion of the menu the day before and he had answered, "It's fine, don't worry, I like most things and I am not a fussy eater." What could have gone wrong? As it turned out, we had a very different definition of 'eat most things'. It looked as if it was most things except for what I had prepared, and not being a fussy eater was certainly debatable.

We ate dinner and watched a couple of films we both enjoyed. Then we went to bed as he was tired. He fell asleep straight away. I didn't. I eventually fell asleep after much pondering of whether this was what I was after. Friendship is nice, but I already had many friends and I hadn't joined an online dating site to find a mate. In the morning, I was woken up but some sort of electronic noises. I tried to ignore them to continue sleeping.

More electronic noises.

This time I opened my eyes, only to realise that the noises were coming from the man next to me. He looking at various videos posted on YouTube on his phone. I wasn't particularly amused by that behaviour and asked: "If you must watch these, could you either turn off the sound if you want to stay in bed or leave the room if you wish to have the sound on." I thought that was a fair compromise.

This had no effect on my companion who continued watching more videos this time on Facebook and the sound was still on, still in bed. I was seriously irritated and snapped: "What the f*ck is wrong with you?" This time, of course, I had sworn and he took notice of me; he got up, got dressed and left the bedroom. Only too late; I couldn't go back to sleep.

I was still furious, not only he had woken me up, but in bed with me on a Sunday morning the only possible thing he could think of doing was checking his Facebook page and watching videos on YouTube? Do you really need your phone in bed in the first place? Anyway, I was awake and went downstairs to sort breakfast. I offered to make coffee, but tea was requested. I got the Tesco's finest tea bags from the top of the cupboard.

"Is that all the tea you have?" he said with a certain disgust in his tone of voice.

"Yes." Not being a tea drinker myself, I have tea, unfortunately not branded.

When people had come around and wanted a cup of tea they hadn't complained about what I had brewed for them. Certainly, no one had used that tone with me.

"If the tea quality is not to standard, there is a shop just across the road if you want to go and get something suitable to your pallate." Not detecting the obvious sarcasm, he said that wouldn't be necessary. Perhaps he was hoping I would go.

I put the kettle on, got the milk out of the fridge for our hot beverages with some cereals and he said, "Is that all the milk you have?"

"Yes, I only drink skimmed milk, again if you want something else the shop is still across the road."

He went on, "You knew I was coming, you could have got some milk I can drink."

Even if I had known what kind of milk he was drinking, I am not sure I would have done so anyway.

I am not in the B&B business and I was brought up to be grateful for what was given to me and thought it applied to everyone else. I stood corrected. He got up, put his shoes on and left the house for the shop, saying he had never seen anyone as rude as me. No? Perhaps you want to try and complain to everything someone does for you and see how they react.

Indeed, I was the rudest person he had ever seen. *[Seriously? I was rude?]* It is true that I swore first thing in the morning, and of course I shouldn't have.

In my defense, I had a pretty bad night's sleep and usually, when people are guests in someone's house they usually accept what is on offer and if it is not to their taste, they are still polite. My friends are, although now I do ask about their preferred taste in tea.

I didn't think that I was that unreasonable.

Then I heard him repeat behind his breath: "I can't believe you have no decent tea and milk nor anything for breakfast, when you know I was coming."

[Am I bad? I also forgot the strip of the red carpet!] Naturally, I was the rude one out of the two of us. He went to the shop came back with some tea, semi-skimmed milk and a couple of crumpets, which he ate without even offering me one.

Then again – no point in sharing, not even offering to share – with someone so rude. Apparently, he had never seen someone that rude (again, got the message the first time), selfish and he was seriously considering not spending the rest of the day with me, as he just couldn't cope with women like that. There was an easy and simple solution to his conundrum and to spare him a lot of consideration, I asked him to leave my house right away.

And he did.

It's complicated.

We need a break away

It was late spring one year and I had been dating someone for a few weeks. It was going well. I had even been introduced to his parents, his friends and I thought, what could possibly go wrong? One evening we were out and he said, 'I think we need a little break away.' I couldn't believe my luck, it sounded quite nice. I thought late summer after the schools have started we could get a good deal.

He said he quite fancied Tenerife as a destination; he went on, adding that one of his friends had a house there and he thought it would be hot and sunny, even in the autumn. I had never been there so I was quite happy to visit a new place.

Over the following weeks, he mentioned the holidays again. Not just to me but to his parents and friends, saying we were going for a little break away in Tenerife later on the in the year. As I had never been there and neither had he, we started asking around for places to stay, things to do, etc… we had eventually agreed on where to stay on the island and I thought it was time for us to put our plan into action.

The following Saturday afternoon, he came to mine and said he wanted to wash his car and I thought I would use that time wisely and book our break away. "When do you fancy going?" I asked to start the booking process.

I got a calendar out and he suggested a week in October. He also mentioned that a whole week may not be convenient to take off at work so we decided on just a long weekend from Wednesday evening to Sunday. To take only two days of annual leave. I looked at my work calendar, that week wasn't ideal for me, as I had a fair few meetings and a training course, but thought, well, I have plenty of time to re-arrange all of that. With that, I entered his chosen dates in the search engine. I enquired about the budget, we agreed that we should keep it reasonable, which I ended up being extremely grateful for.

I started looking at the search results came through and asked whether he preferred half board, B&B or all-inclusive. "B&B," he answered. "It would be nice to walk in the evening and find our own restaurant."

I agreed with that idea and searched for a B&B and he went to the drive and started to wash his car. I went on with the search and looked at accommodation, flights, transfers, etc. I found a few suitable hotels at a reasonable price – there was a choice of three – so I called him back inside for a minute in and asked which one he preferred. After a little glance, he chose one. We were all good to go, ready, steady, book.

I paid the deposit with my credit card for the two of us. We hadn't booked too much in advance, so the remainder of the hotel was due shortly after that and I mentioned the breakaway and said, "We'll need to pay the rest shortly. Anything else you want to add to our holiday: hire a car, etc?"

"No," he answered. "Go ahead I'll pay you later." With that statement, I concluded the booking.

When my credit card statement arrived a few weeks later, I sent him a message saying that the break away payment was due and asked how he wanted to pay for his half. His answer came as a bit of a blow. He said he wasn't going as he didn't have a valid passport. To say it was a bit of a shock would be the understatement of the year! I must confess it is not often that someone suggests going away on a break in a FOREIGN country and letting me book, knowing full well that he did not have a passport. Not letting myself be beaten down, I immediately thought the break was not for a while, so there is still plenty of time to apply for a renewal.

"Are you going to renew your passport?" I enquired.

"Am too busy at work for that."

"What is happening about our break away?"

No answer, and the subject was changed for the evening. The next day I tried again. After all, he was busy at work so thought it best to wait until the evening to ask again. We didn't have any plans to meet and I knew he wasn't going out so thought he may be able to find some time to go online and renew his passport.

"Hello, how are you? Still at work?" I enquired tentatively.

"No just chilling."

"Excellent," I thought, "nothing much to occupy his mind." I went on, "Are you going to renew your passport this evening?"

"I need someone to countersign the form."

"I know but this shouldn't be a major issue, no?"

"My friend who can do it is on holiday, but I'll ask him when he is back."

A few days later, when said friend was meant to be back, I followed through with another text: "Have you spoken to your friend about your passport?"

"Not yet."

I left it again for a couple of days. By then, not only had I paid my bill, but it was also getting very near the time where I couldn't even change the name of my companion, because if all failed I still had friends that could still come and join me. We had both been busy at work and hadn't had a chance to meet again and talk about the holiday.

I asked again, "Have you renewed your passport? If not, let me know so that I can change your name to someone else's?"

"Yes, it was all renewed and sent yesterday so I should have it just in time for the departure."

I was relieved. The passport story had stressed me out and I was in need of a breakaway! I asked for the money again and never had an answer. I was wondering if he was still intending to come. "Of course!" he maintained. "Looking forward to it."

I wasn't so sure. I made a few enquiries but by then it was too late to change anything and the airline wasn't going to refund me anything or let me change the names on the tickets, even if I could find someone to come along. I was feeling extremely nervous about this holiday. A couple of days before departure, I asked for the money again he answered: "Well, I have asked for those two days and my boss has not allowed my time off."

I was pretty mad at that time. Most people would have been, I am sure. I couldn't believe what was happening. I originally thought, "not to worry, I'll find someone to come with me." I phoned the airline to see if I could amend the booking but I was told it was too late for that and a refund wasn't an option as the tickets were non-exchangeable and non-refundable.

Great! At the price they were, I thought the exchangeable would have been an option.

I had a couple of days to ponder whether I would go on my own or not. It was not the solo type of holiday I was familiar with. Solo, yes, but usually they are with many other singletons and with lots of fun. I was going to be on my own and have to make my own entertainment.

On the other hand, staying at home and wasting all that money sounded daft too. I decided to phone the hotel and I was luckier with them. They offered to amend my booking from a double to a single and instead offered me half board instead of B&B. Things were looking up. It is one thing strolling in a foreign land in the evening hand in hand with your partner to find a place to eat, but on your own, it is a little intimidating.

A few days later I was on my way to Tenerife. The sun was shining, the pool was amazing and quiet. I made full used of the hotel gym and spa. The area was beautiful and the staff was absolutely brilliant. I may have been on my own, but they certainly went out of their way to make my stay a memorable one.

At breakfast, the waiter came with the evening menu where I could select my food in advance. Come the evening, I was served within minutes after sitting down and I never had to wait too long for my second course and never found myself in the restaurant looking and feeling awkward in a room full of people. It was truly a wonderful break away and glad I decided to go.

Looking back at this episode I can't help but wonder:

- ♀ Do you really leave it to the last minute to book your annual leave? Of course not.
- ♀ Are a couple of days in the scheme of things really that hard to take? Of course not. No one is that indispensable.
- ♀ What kind of moron would suggest a break away abroad without a passport?

It's complicated.

My wife has my credit card

Another profile, another local gentleman.

We met for evening meals, nights out in London, walks on Sunday afternoons. We were having an enjoyable time and it was all very friendly.

The only thing was everything was a little unpredictable as he had said: "It's a little complicated."

I knew he had left his wife and he was living on his own. It was a different kind of complication. Everything was last minute. He was meant to see his kids, then I would receive a phone call: "Are you free to go for a drink?" Or he had planned some activities with his children on Saturday, then when the Saturday afternoon came, it was a sunny day and thought he has a nice weather for his afternoon with his kids, then the phone rang: "Do you fancy an ice cream?"

We met in town had an ice cream and we went for a walk, etc. He hadn't seen his kids. He never saw his kids. They always cancelled at the last minute. I felt for him for not seeing his kids but there was little I could help with in that respect. On the rare occasions, we did manage to do something or go somewhere together, he never had any money, yet he had a decent enough job.

We continued our impromptu meetings and he was always telling me about his ideal woman, who I must say, was very very similar to me, frighteningly so. Yet he never tried anything. He claimed to only want friendship, which for a while seemed OK. I was filling the void of some lonely evenings, sharing a meal was way more sociable than just eating on your own.

What was incredible – and the reason he was so unpredictable – was that when he left his wife, which had been three or four years previously, he had left her his credit cards. I must say that it did make me laugh when I found out. Why on earth would you do that? There were some serious unresolved issues here. Guilt, possibly?

The irony in our discussions was that he didn't mind telling me how to deal with my ex. Always telling me what I should do and yet his wife had his credit cards. Let me tell you, she wasn't shy about using them! Another one who despite the separation a few years previously, hadn't thought divorce was a priority. Incredible!

Which self-respecting woman would think that you are serious about her when you are still legally and financially bound to someone else?

It's complicated.

Not allowed a bad day

There are days where you shouldn't get out of bed! It was one of these days. I was due to go for a second opinion at the Moorfields eye hospital. I was losing vision in one eye and wanted a second opinion to establish whether there was anything that could be done for me rather than wait till it got better.

I woke up in the morning, arrived in my bathroom only to realise that my two-day-old shower hadn't been fixed properly. I started the day wondering how I was going to sort it out. I had to find a new plumber fairly fast. The morning dragged as I was worried about what the second opinion would reveal and trying to ascertain how not to be ripped off again by a new plumber. The time of the appointment was looming and my friend came to pick me up to give me a lift to the station. I needed to take the train to London, as train and tube seemed to be the easiest option when you can't see very well. I only needed a lift to the station and back, rather than a lift to the hospital.

The appointment went well, although I was told I required some paperwork. Naturally, no one had bothered telling me it was needed BEFORE the appointment. By that time, my pupils were dilated, I couldn't see anything, so had to ring friends to search and complete the paperwork on my behalf. You would have thought that being an eye hospital, preparing the paperwork prior to someone becoming temporarily blind would have been logical. It all got resolved in the end and I was making my way back home.

I had just started dating a new man and he had kindly offered to pick me up from the train station after work and to cook for me. I thought it was really kind of him to offer. Since I knew I wouldn't be able to see much, the idea of not dealing with hot water and gas for the evening was terribly tempting. I was grateful for someone to help me out. I was hoping he would actually cook, as I am not a fan of processed food. It wasn't my day and he arrived with a ready meal and went along with prepared food to be put in the oven. Beggars can't be choosers.

As the dish was warming in the oven, I realised that I had forgotten to put the dishwasher on in the morning and it was full, so I put it on. Press the button and heard an almighty BANG.

And it never started.

I was down from a tough day and when it got worse – shower, dishwasher, little sleep the previous night – I felt really down. My boyfriend piped up and said, "I am here and you are horrible to me, so I am going to go as soon as I have eaten." I enquired how I had been horrible to HIM? I was genuinely interested in knowing how it had become all about him and how I was 'horrible'. It seemed a little extreme to me.

Apparently, he was there and I was not in a good mood, hence me being horrible. Thanks for your understanding and kicking me while I am down. As if his presence alone should be sufficient to wave all my problems goodbye! Seeing his cheery little face should always make me smile! How could I be so heartless? It is not as if I had a bad day or anything.

With tears on my face, I said, "If you want to go, be my guest." If he was only here for the good times, that day wasn't one of them, so he was correct, he should certainly go. Anyway, we shared the meal he had put in the oven to heat up with me. He decided against going home after dinner, despite me being horrid to him and in a mood and he suggested we should watch a film.

The distraction couldn't have been more welcome! He chose a film and twenty minutes in, he fell asleep on the sofa. He asked if I minded, but he needed to go to sleep and he went upstairs and slept like a baby all night; he left in the morning for work without saying a word.

Considering his lack of understanding and support, his thrilling company and calling me horrible, it became a memorable night all round but not for the right reasons!

It's complicated.

Best advice
I had started seeing someone who lived on the coast and one evening I was making my way down to spend the

weekend with him. I had just reached the motorway when one of my dashboard lights started to flash. Not what you want to see at the beginning of a car journey. I had this problem before, it was merely telling me that one or more tyres were losing pressure, becoming flat and obviously I needed to see to it.

I decided to stop at the first petrol station on the way to investigate which tyre was causing the issue. Then, if possible, blow it back to its normal pressure or change it, if I had a puncture. I stopped and looked around and couldn't see anything wrong with any of my tyres. The air machine was out of order and I wasn't quite sure what to do next.

It was 22.30 and dark. Luckily it wasn't raining. I was halfway between my house and my final destination and was debating whether it would be easier to make my way back home or to continue. In a moment of madness, I decided to call my boyfriend to explain that I was either going to be late or not turn up and also wanted a bit of advice as to whether I was endangering myself and others. I naively phoned and explained my situation.

At that time of night, he was in the pub with his mates and I detected a slight slurring of words, which he denied: "Just had a couple" he said. *[Most probably bottles but hey.]*

One thing was certain: he wasn't coming to help me. I explained that the light had started to flash, but I couldn't see that a tyre was flat and as a result, I was not sure what the trouble was.

His answer was insightful: "If it ain't flat, it ain't flat. See which one is flat and change it." As it happened, if one of my tyres required changing I had just had a manicure and changing the tyre was certainly not an option. Thankfully, I have my car rescue card which I barely used. I pay a fairly large sum every year, so now would have been the time to actually use the services. To be honest, ten years of premium payment for a flat tyre, cannot be considered the most cost-effective way to change a tyre but that wasn't the point.

He was still at the other end of the phone telling me to change the tyre. I couldn't see which tyre had lost pressure and whether or not it needed to be changed, it could have just required more air. My arguments were futile. He suggested that I should ask the guy at the till in the petrol station to help me change the tyre. If only I knew which tyre required changing that would have been a great idea.

Looking at the petrol station staff, I had been in there earlier about the air machine not working and the person inside the shop was no more than sixteen and with as much customer service flair as a toothbrush and possibly just as experienced as me in wheel changing. I was giving up. Bearing in mind I still wasn't sure what to do, I knew I would figure it out since helpful advice wasn't forthcoming from the Man Camp. I told them that I was going to arrive later than first anticipated. I must confess that I have heard a few stupid comments in my life but never to the level of what was to come.

It was at this point that boyfriend surpassed himself and suggested for me to stand by the side of the road and wait for a middle-aged man to stop and offer to help me change the tyre. I put the phone down. There is also a name for women who stand by the side of the road at night waiting for men.

Thanks for that, it was really helpful advice, I'll sort myself out.

It's complicated.

Workaholic

It was time to try another website. Hoping for better luck. Again!

Over the years I tried a few and went back to some with the same level of success, but it is a mystery to me how 'comparethedatingwebsite.com' manage to get their ratings and their testimonies. At times I seemed to be the only one having disastrous encounters. Anyway, I tried that site again despite the fact that it was dearer, hoping once again that the price factor alone would be a time waster deterrent. Not necessarily the case.

On this particular website you couldn't search for a match, the system did that for you, and it was more often than not a complete mystery on why the computer had matched you with a particular person. I started corresponding with someone who lived outside London but who worked in London. I thought it would be convenient to meet halfway in London and, let's face it, you can't be short of a thing or two to do in the capital city.

His profile looked truly interesting. He seemed to have many hobbies, he had travelled. It was encouraging. We should have lots to talk about. First few emails were enjoyable. He was telling me about his children, holidays, his house abroad and what it was like over there. We eventually decided to meet after work one day in London. It was a fine restaurant – probably one of the better one I had been taken to, difficult to find – I got lost many times on my way there – but excellent.

We had a great time. I told him about me, as you always do on a first date. After the meal, he confessed he hadn't laughed so much in ages… laughing with me, of course, since I only mentioned things that had happened to me. I felt I had monopolised the conversation, but he seemed to have enjoyed it. We decided to meet again, in London, so I travelled to London one day after work. We met near the train station, which was handy but the meal was absolutely foul – not to mention expensive – which certainly didn't make me laugh. I found out just how expensive afterwards when I paid for my share of the meal. Quite honestly, it was an overpriced basic meal, poorly cooked and badly presented. I shall make sure never to go there again.

The face to face encounter was going the same way as during our phone conversations: how busy the day had been, the weather. Nothing much to write home about. The few chats we had on the phone were over relatively quickly. Besides his work and description of where he had stayed that week *[he was travelling a lot]*, there was little else he discussed.

From his conversations, I understood that he was a big cheese in a company. I got it, long hours, places to travel too, hotels, restaurants and little else and it showed. During that meal, I felt a strong sense of déja-vu. At the end of the day, you take the train somewhere, go to meetings, stay in hotel new meetings and travel back; it doesn't matter how much you do that in a week, at the third trip, you are bored! I know, I have been there myself and I was travelling abroad, whereas his trips were the only UK-based.

The glamour of travelling for work soon wears off even more so when you relate it to someone else. I enquired what he did at the weekends: "Nothing much but caught up on some work." *[Obviously. What else could you be doing at the weekend besides work?!]* "I see," I added and with those words, his side of the dialogue ended.

I told him about my plans for the coming weeks: theatre, plays, outings, etc., but I am not sure I had his full interest there. He said he wasn't going out much because he was travelling a lot and couldn't plan too much and didn't have much time because of work commitments. *[Don't try and make yourself too exciting, will you?]* I tried to speak about his forthcoming holiday.

It was getting into the winter months and I read on his profile that he was into skiing. Something we both had in common. He told me he had some holidays booked, so tried to engage in a new discussion where we could both contribute and perhaps eventually both enjoy together.

"When is your next skiing holiday?" I asked, trying to get a bit more enthusiasm out of him.

"Going to France for a long weekend."

"Exciting. Where?"

"France." *[As if I hadn't got it the first time, France is a big place!]*

"Where in France?" I am starting to feel like the Spanish Inquisition. Is this so difficult?

"Avoriaz."

"Avoriaz is a great resort, I have skiied there before. We were blessed by brilliant snow and sunshine. Have you been there before?"

"No."

"Looking forward to it?"

"Yes."

[Wonderful!] With this engaging banter I decided to give up on my Spanish Inquisition technique and concentrate on the food on my plate. I realised he hadn't spoken much on the first date and wanted to let him open up a bit, but without much success.

I ended up giving him the benefit of the doubt and putting his lack of response down to a bad day. These things happen, besides, no reason to conclude to anything else since outside our meeting I had a decent amount of text messages and phone calls. Looking back, they were all pretty concise.

He went on his holiday and we carried on messaging

each other. It was nice and we decided to meet up again when we were both back from our respective trips. I also had a skiing holiday booked. The week we were back, we met up again and we ended up having yet another overpriced dinner after work in London. At least the food was decent that time.

Since we had both been away, I thought there may be a little tale to tell, a few skiing anecdotes, perhaps. He didn't seem to have any or none that he was prepared to share with me. With that, he became the only person I knew who didn't have anything to say about his skiing week.

That third rendezvous had me looking at my watch. He turned out to be a bit of a bore, talking mainly about his work, if I had related to it, it could have been OK. I didn't and it wasn't.

It ended up being a disappointment after such a promising profile. Unfortunately, 'Go Compare' exists for dating but sadly doesn't come with trade description protection!

It is complicated.

I don't know what I want

Once I was contacted by a new 'potential' lifelong partner who lived in Yorkshire. Easily five hours' drive from where I lived. However, the emails were very nice, so I answered. When you are home alone it is always pleasant to find an email in your inbox; it keeps you occupied for that evening. Sometimes the sender came from abroad, but this one came from Yorkshire. I was a bit puzzled as to why he seemed so keen to know more about me, but my curiosity took over and I answered.

We started chatting. I really liked his style, his anecdotes, etc., what he had to say. He was clearly cultured and educated and I came to look forward to his emails, they were always so interesting. I didn't think much would come of it as he lived so far away, you could hardly meet for coffee when it's a five-hour commute each way!

We resumed our 'pen pal' kind of relationship and then one day he rang.

"What you are up to?" he asked cheerfully.

"Not much," I replied.

"OK, then I am driving to you."

He explained that he had been visiting a family member and could be driving to me – should be there in three to four hours if the traffic is good. I offered to book him a hotel room nearby for him to stay. I was looking forward to seeing him in the flesh. I was seriously excited, a bit worried by a full day long first date, but thought what the hell, it could be nice.

And it was. We spent the weekend together, talked, and laughed. It was brilliant. He explained that his life was at a crossroads. His wife and he had split up but decided to stay together until their youngest went to university a few months from then. He had plans to sell the business him and his wife had together and a new chapter of his life was literally starting and was not decided on where in the country this would be.

He was very upbeat, had lots of interests, plenty to talk about and very interesting too. A very good first date. The beauty of it is that he was down for the weekend and stayed at a hotel nearby and we could meet again the very next day. I thoroughly enjoyed the weekend. On the Sunday afternoon, he went back to Yorkshire and we emailed on a daily basis, followed by the occasional text. We sent each other pictures of our favourite places, discussing where he had been, where we would like to go, it was all so fine.

A couple of weeks later, he came back to see me and it was just brilliant. The conversation was flowing, we had so much in common, affinity was just good. We laughed, time flew by. I was starting to think this was going very well indeed. I did ask why he had contacted me and why someone so far away? He explained that he had thought about it and wanted to start afresh where there would not be any connection with people him and his children knew. He said he had approached the subject with his youngest and he had replied that he was OK with his parents splitting up but wouldn't be able to handle if his dad was going to date the mother of some friends at school. I thought it was a fair explanation.

Since he was selling his business in Yorkshire and looking for a new job elsewhere in the country, Kent seemed just as good a place as any. That sounded like an excellent and very plausible answer. Besides, I am extremely gullible.

During our day together, I mentioned that it was a bit of a pain not being able to talk on the phone. The reception was poor where he lived and although we talked daily, it was always cutting off, so I suggested to ring his landline. To which he answered that his wife still lived with him. It came as a bit of a shock, but still being married doesn't stop you from speaking on the phone to people, besides, he had said he was divorced. Or had I missed something?

Yes yes yes, of course he was divorced. The decree nisi was out but the decree absolute was just about to come out when the business had been sold. I tried to enquire about the sale of the business. From all accounts, it didn't seem such an easy task to me. He assured me that all was falling into place and it was only a matter of a few weeks at the most. "Mmmm, so maybe not as divorced as he claimed to have been," I thought to myself. Especially if phoning people from the landline is prohibited. I wasn't too impressed with that answer but surely a small set back, I reassured myself, as the rest was lovely. So just a temporary setback, I hoped.

Following that weekend, we renewed our correspondence, mainly via emails. Then he happily announced that he had found a place where we could facetime. It made our communication much better. We facetimed daily.

As he lived in Yorkshire and I had some holiday left I suggested renting a cottage near him to be a little closer for a few days. It sounded much better than facetiming and a brilliant idea to me. Not so much to him. "Too close for comfort," he said. I wasn't quite sure too close from what but clearly too close.

A week passed and another and then another. I wondered if we were going to see each other anytime soon or is this going to remain mostly a paper relationship.

I asked, "When are you planning to come over next, since my idea of going nearer to you wasn't viable?"

His answer came as a bit of a shock: "Well you know it is a long way?"

"Indeed. Do you remember me querying it as soon as you started communicating with me and you assured me that this was not a problem, and convinced me four to five hours' drive wasn't much has you were used to driving that kind of distance? Hence your first few visits."

A new answer came quickly though: "I need to look after the pets."

"Can't your wife, friend or neighbour do that? You told me your wife recently went away for a week; surely you could go away for another weekend? Who looked after them when you last came over previously?"

"She did."

"She can't do it again?"

"I also have to look after my dad. He is getting old and not very mobile, so I look after him at the weekend."

"Very commendable. What happened last time you came to see me?"

"And I have other commitments."

"Like?"

"Well, as you know, I am studying to go back to work."

"Mmmm, also when there's a will there's a way, again, it didn't seem to be so vital last time." Somehow, I didn't feel the will was there any longer. It became apparent that the list of excuses was becoming longer and longer.

This was mid-January by that time and we had been communicating since December with two visits in two weeks during that first month. Considering the distance, the animals, the father and the other commitments it was a real achievement. It was getting close to five weeks since our last meeting and I was wondering if he was one of those guys that was still married and where their divorce is only a figment of their imagination.

At the end of January, he promised he would come over for Valentine's Day. It was another two weeks to wait, and I thought a Valentine's weekend sounded delightful. I bought a card and a book as a little present as he confessed that reading was one of his guilty pleasures. I thought he might especially enjoy that one. I didn't want to spend too much time and effort on Valentine's gifts, as I was almost convinced he wasn't going to come over. We spent those two weeks communicating, texting and emailing as usual.

The second week, I had booked a week's skiing and despite the terrible Wi-Fi in the hotel, we managed to make contact daily. We were all set for Valentine's Day. The day I returned home.

The last night of my holiday, I texted him: "Looking forward to tomorrow. I'll probably feel worse for wear in the morning on the bus to the airport as we have been celebrating our last evening in Austria with some pretty strong schnapps. Can't wait to see you again tomorrow evening."

I was taken aback by the answer: "Do you still want me to come?"

"Of course, what sort of question is that?"

"Not sure after reading your text."

I read my message again. Sometimes you end up typing something you don't strictly mean. Nothing controversial in my text and certainly nothing to suggest I had changed my mind in any way. I continued my message by saying: "Where is that coming from?"

"I wonder if you still want me to come over."

Really?

The 'I can't wait to see you again' part of my text must have been confusing to him. This changed my mood and I followed with, "If you don't want to come, don't, but I haven't changed my mind. Let me know what you decide." I left my friends at the bar of the hotel and went to bed.

The next morning, I got up and looked at my phone. No message, no answer back. Unusual, as I always used to have a 'good morning' text every day. I was expecting something like 'have a safe journey home' or something to that effect. Nothing. At the airport, I logged onto my phone with free airport Wi-Fi, still nothing from him. I sent a text: 'Hope you are OK, haven't heard from you today. About to go on a plane now. Text me when you leave Yorkshire so that I can work out an ETA for you.'

I flew back, drove home, still nothing.

I phoned – no answer.

I texted – no answer

I emailed: "I presume from lack of answers that you are no longer coming."

I received an answer in my inbox seconds later: "Well I was going to come but there's a problem with the water so I had to ring a plumber." What a poor excuse! I went on with his explanation and said: "If you had a problem with water at home all the more reason for you to come to mine for the weekend and let your wife ring the plumber. She'll need to get used to sort things out on her own when you are no longer together."

"I couldn't let her do that."

"Couldn't tell her to ring a plumber?"

"She wouldn't know which one."

"Yellow pages, trust a trader, friends' recommendations, internet? How difficult must it be to call a plumber?"

"I cannot expect her to ring."

Obviously not. Then came the coup de grace: "I thought you didn't want me there."

"How so?"

"I don't know."

There's no answer to that.

Why can't you just man up and say, "I no longer want to come." Would it not be easier than keeping on making up excuses? If you are still half married, living miles away with your (ex) wife, you have animals, commitments, your old dad to look after, why on earth did you even start contacting me and wasting my time and messing with my feelings?

It's complicated.

God's gift keeps on giving

This time, I was contacted by someone who wouldn't have ordinarily been my first choice. Looking at the profile hadn't convinced me that we would be a match either. Not judging a book from his cover – after all, he could have been kind, considerate, thoughtful, interesting or witty – we met. Although it was too early to decide on his personal attributes, I realised, to my surprise, that we had similar views on a number of things and we had quite a lot to talk about. This made a refreshing change and I thought it was promising.

We never met very much because he had half custody of his children and when he was with them there was no contact with me. In the early days, I certainly understand that you want to get used to each other before you start adding your children to the equation. I understood that perfectly. I always did that with my own daughters and since his were younger, I certainly approved. Besides I had my hobbies, so half the time, when he was busy with his children I was busy too, so it was all good. We had the odd lunchtime rendezvous before the school run and evening meals every now and then.

As I was getting to know him over the phone, some of his discussions became a little alarming as well as terribly entertaining and couldn't leave it at that. He certainly knew how to arouse my curiosity and continued to see him.

He once told me that he used to swing with his wife and that, clearly, him and her were never short of partners as they were the best-looking couple. Modesty is a virtue. I didn't know his wife, but I could see him and although he was nice looking enough, he was no George Clooney and he was seriously overweight.

He went on saying that all the women were after him as he could give them multiple orgasms in no time, and the word got around. I thought perhaps be they were just gasping for air if he was on top... easy mistake to make! Needless to say I kept that to myself but he made me smile nevertheless. The thought of swinging does not appeal to me at all. And if he was the best these parties offered, I am comforted in the thought that I am not missing much by not participating!

Thinking of that conversation, did he really need to mention it to me? Do you really want to spice things up when you haven't even started? Could his wife possibly be looking for an easy and legitimate way to have sex with someone else without hurting his feelings?

I know I can be cynical. I wasn't quite sure why he wanted to share that with me so early on, perhaps to entice me. Who knows? Clearly, I was onto a sure thing! And so was he! Surely not getting very far with me. Maybe he was just teasing me and trying to get a reaction.

We continued messaging and talking on the phone. He went on a family holiday and we started WhatsApping, enjoying the free communicating across countries at no costs!

One of the conversations when he was on holiday lead to him telling me that he had a hot tub at home. I am not a huge fan of hot tubs at the best of times. To me it would feel odd to have a bath outside the bathroom and share it with all sorts of people, but hey! He also declared that at his house there were no swimsuits worn in the hot tub. Even worse.

He eventually came back from holiday and we saw each other for a couple of times. During one of our drinks, he said he was considering going on holiday with a girlfriend of his. I didn't see a problem with that, I too had a holiday booked with friends in the near future. Then he added, "She is a girlfriend of mine. She is just a friend, she is too fat for me." Not quite sure what he was alluding to and why he had to make that last statement. As far as I am concerned, my friends are friends and not potential partners and I am not passing comments on their size.

He carried on by saying, "You are just right, but don't put on any more weight, I like my woman to look good and if you put on weight I'll dump you." Charming! Quite the gentleman too! Another one who dared to describe himself as a romantic on his profile. Looking back at his profile, he had put down 'average build'. That was debatable.

I wasn't sure how to take the warning about keeping my weight to what it was and without thinking much about my answer I said, 'It's the pot calling the kettle black a bit, no?'

"Are you saying I am fat?" he replied defensively.

I was trying not to say that actually but considering his previous comment, the gloves were almost off. I may have a couple of kilos I could get rid of, but in his case, it was more a couple of stones!

"You are not exactly skinny, are you? There are mirrors and scales in your house, right?"

No answer.

Perhaps I was not exactly subtle but telling me not to put on weight was not exactly sensitive either!

Having accepted the fact that we were both insensitive, we carried on speaking and messaging. Unfortunately, the meeting up was always problematic. We eventually agreed to meet up for lunch.

"I'll pick you up upon returning to the garage where my car is being serviced," he explained. "We'll have lunch before the school run."

It sounded like a reasonable plan.

11.30am. He texted me saying he'd be over soon, he needed to wash his car.

In my case, when I say I need to wash my car, I mean someone else is doing it whilst I am carrying on my normal day. If I decide to sit and wait at the car wash, it takes around ten minutes. Generally, washing my car doesn't interfere with my planned activities. In his case, he did it himself and it took till about 13.30 when he asked me when I was coming over, as there won't be much time left before I leave for school?

I was still expecting him to pick me up and therefore made myself a sandwich; lunch wasn't going to happen. Apparently, I had misread the message. He had never said he would pick me up, I was to meet him at his. The message was still on my phone, I re-read it and it still read, "I'll pick you up." Misreading it a second time.

I was free the following weekend, and so was he. He had told me so earlier that week. I thought it would be the ideal opportunity to spend more time together and get to know each other a little better than a stolen hour here and there and make the best use of a free weekend by perhaps doing something together. No suggestions were forthcoming during the week and ended up suggesting that we could do something together at the weekend.

"I am going away for the weekend."

I was clearly not part of his weekend plans so I went on with my life and organised something with one of my friends. At 21.30 on the Sunday evening, the phone rang and I picked up.

"I am on my way back. Thought I could come over?"

"A bit of notice would have been nice, I am watching TV in bed."

"I'll come and join you."

[Nice try.]

"How was your weekend?"

"I saw an acquaintance, she really fancies me!"

"Does she now?" *[What a surprise! Would any woman be strong enough to resist?]*

"That's the price you have to pay for being irresistible, I am afraid," I stated jokingly.

The conversation was short and let him go back to his own place. I am made of strong stuff and was able to resist. We agreed to meet during the week. Twice he cancelled at the last minute as he had emergencies. The first time was a work problem and the second was an issue with the ex. At the second cancellation, we didn't rearrange to see each other again. To tell the truth, I wasn't holding my breath. Later on that week, I was off work and busy on household chores and I get a message at lunchtime: "Come and meet me." It was gone 13.00 and over an hour away so I declined the offer. I knew he would have to do the school run at 14.45. I didn't fancy two hours' drive for a forty-five-minute meeting, no matter how heavenly the meeting.

"I thought it would be spontaneous," he said.

"Sounds more like an afterthought to me."

Although it was difficult to meet, we were talking on the phone most days and it was a form of company. General chitchatting is good just to forget about the stress of your day. One of these days, I had a hospital appointment for my eye. I hadn't made a fuss about it, I knew the drill and it was just a check-up. I had dinner with my daughter and after dinner, he rang me.

I thought 'bless', he remembered and is enquiring how it went. I couldn't be further from the truth. He hadn't remembered. The only reason he rang was to tell me that he had rung his ex that afternoon and they had had a huge row. I thought, "Well you tell me about your day and I tell you about mine." These things usually went like that. I let him tell me the blow by blow of his argument and she said that and he answered that she wasn't happy, what does she think? Stupid mare! And then she said this. And he said that. Etc, etc. It went on for forty minutes. My ear was starting to ache.

I was really sorry that he didn't have 10p to ring someone who might have been interested in every detail of the argument with his ex. Sadly, telephone boxes are a thing of the past. To cut a long (too long) story short, they were going to court. How so? Surely there must have been other ways to resolve the issue. Oh no. Not with HER, she is sooooo unreasonable.

I enquired, "Have you considered not answering the phone when she rings, or if an argument starts you just make your excuses and save yourself an argument? It takes a minimum of two people to argue." Apparently, I couldn't understand. What I couldn't understand is why he let her and why he felt the need to relive the experience with me!

Naturally, I had started the conversation all sympathetic, but after twenty minutes my patience ran thin and I was starting to wonder why on earth you would want to tell your potential new girlfriend about the petty little arguments you still have with your ex after years of splitting up. It certainly doesn't make you sound like someone who can let go, someone with a grudge, and I could go on. Nor does it highlight your best side.

Eventually, the phone call ended: "She is just incredible, anyway I must go, I need to cook tea and I am going out later." He put the phone down. [Yes, and my day was fine, thanks for asking.] Truth be told, I was relieved that phone call was over.

During one of our many chats, he had boasted about being a mean cook which had prompted me to ask when I was going to have the honour of tasting his culinary delights. I didn't mention the hot tub. I certainly didn't fancy any of that! I was told that I could never come to his place because of his lodgers, two girls I was told, who he only had to say a word and he would be 'in there' *[I am sure]* but he had told them they couldn't bring anyone home, therefore, he couldn't receive anyone either. *[Did he actually think I was buying that?]* I was a little alarmed about everyone not wearing swimwear in the hot tub with the lodgers, etc. I didn't ask; I really didn't want to know. I couldn't go to his place and I wasn't too keen on having him around either.

With hindsight, I should have cut it short as it quickly became a waste of time. A few phone calls, some not always enjoyable, an occasional meeting here and then: no harm was being done, coupled with bad judgment, I decided to carry on. In the end, it was a good idea as he provided me with some good material for this book.

It was actually difficult to meet and at the time this took place, I was about to go on holiday with my friends. Me, twelve months prior with eight of my friends, him with a friend that can only go on holiday with him as she feels safe with him, but a little too fat for him to fancy her, as he had kindly highlighted to me before, a holiday that he was just organising.

As he kept on complaining that I wasn't making any effort to see him, I thought that he might have perhaps organised his holiday at the same time as mine. I was incorrect and he organised it for the week I came back, which wasn't too logical to me. I still can't understand why he moaned about my holiday. Anyway, our holidays would mean another two weeks without being able to meet.

I suggested that we should maybe do something the weekend he came back, which turned out not to be possible as that weekend he would be with his children. So potential new date was postponed to four weeks' time. I must admit, I wasn't holding my breath and couldn't see why he thought I was the one not making any effort to see him.

During the holidays, the texting got a little disrupted but he managed to send me a picture of him, *[of course]* where he was clearly holding his breath in and displaying breasts most teenage girls would be proud to have! "Well well well," I thought. "Someone has certainly enjoyed his food during that week." It made me smile in the light of his earlier comment.

Our holidays came to an end and we attempted to meet again the following week on Tuesday. Unfortunately, I had to go abroad on business and stay over for one night. Business needs prevailing, my night away happened to be on that very same Tuesday. Once again, he moaned and complained, saying I was never there and was never able to make time for him, as if I could dictate my workload to suit him. He had clearly forgotten about all the dates he had cancelled at the last minute. (Four if I counted correctly! Only he wasn't counting his cancellations, only the one I had to postpone for work. Double standards or what?)

I suggested another night that week. None of which were convenient for him. He was busy both weekends and every night that week except for the Tuesday. How unreasonable of me to be working the only day he was free to see me! He finished with, "Well, ring me when you are back," and he put the phone down. As if I could help my work demands. The business trip took place and I caught a massive chest infection on the plane. I ended up off sick for a week and, sadly, hadn't rung His Majesty as soon as I landed.

I received a text saying, "I thought you were going to ring as soon as you were back!"

"I was, but have a chest infection so in bed with paracetamol. My trip went well, thanks for asking!"

He didn't see the sarcasm in that last comment. I added that I was expecting to be better in a couple of days and we agreed to go for a meal then. He chose the day and I agreed.

The day finally arrived. I was grateful for going out and not eating on my own. I was getting ready when I received a text: "I have started seeing someone and I want to pursue that."

"*That?* Interesting choice of word," I thought. I can't say I was at all surprised. 'That' was one lucky lady!

It's complicated.

Love me, love my dogs

The dating was going great. We had lots and lots in common, came from the same area, liked the same singers, same films, same food. It was just brilliant. Such a fabulous change. Thought, "YES! May it carry on!" One evening, he invited me and cooked one of my favourite meals. From previous conversations we had, I knew he cooked and was expecting the meal to be all homemade. Happy days.

As I arrived at his place, I noticed he had two dogs, fairly cute as far as dogs are concerned, but dogs nevertheless. He warned me to keep my shoes on and to walk around with care as one of his dogs was young and was not house trained yet and I could be walking in anything... Nice!

We had dinner and he didn't disappoint. The food was truly delicious. I enjoyed his company very much even if towards the end of the meal the conversation already started to turn to the ex. On a third date, it was a bit too heavy for me but hey, I was getting used to it – we all have a past – and let him make the best use of my listening skills.

Meanwhile, the dogs started to make me sneeze and my throat was burning. Luckily, I had some antihistamine and the evening continued in a pleasant way. After dinner, I left, avoiding the pool of dog wee in the hallway. I had been warned. I had kept my shoes on and didn't have to clean the mess after all.

A few days later, I invited him to watch one of our favourite films at home. A few minutes before leaving his place he rings me and said, "Can my dogs come too?" [*What the dogs that are not house trained?*] I said not. He came, we watched the film, he left and I never heard from him again.

It's complicated.

Sorry

For a period of eighteen months of my life, I had an eye problem. Nothing sinister, but it was a massive irritation and it gave me nasty headaches at times. I had to rely on my daughters to take me to hospital and back as I couldn't drive, but I knew it was not going to be permanent and that it would get back to normal in the end. It was nothing serious, it just needed time and patience for it to heal.

It was one of these days that was the onset of the problem. I had been on a few dates over a period of four to five weeks with a new gentleman. I had spent a huge part of my day mostly waiting for my turn at the hospital but was looking forward to my evening as we had arranged to go out on that Friday evening. Just what the doctor ordered!

I felt rather disheartened at work following the hospital appointment and literally couldn't wait to leave and go home and go out. Finally, going home time arrived and I went home. I showered and started to get ready. I was expecting a text message at any moment telling me where and when to meet.

It had been a busy day for both of us and we hadn't messaged, but since we had agreed to go out on the Friday evening the previous evening, I was convinced I would hear from him very soon.

I came out of the shower: nothing.

I messaged, "Ready when you are."

I started to sort out the laundry, tidied a few bits in the kitchen, then I sent another message, "What are the plans for this evening?"

Still no answer.

Then my mobile phone rang. It was him. He announced that he was going out with his mates this evening and wouldn't be seeing me.

I don't know whether I was more angry or surprised by his actions. I asked if I could join him and his friends since I had already met them; it wasn't as if it was all new or awkward.

I added that following the day I had, I was really keen to get out of the house, let my hair down and have a good evening.

"I know," he agreed, "but tonight I am not seeing you."

I was not best pleased by the turn of events. To make matters worse, by the time he rang, it was far too late to arrange anything with anyone else. He must have organised his meeting with his mates during the day and it would have been the most basic level of politeness to actually let me know a little earlier so that I could have organised something else.

"I'll come around tomorrow and we can do something during the day."

"OK then, speak tomorrow."

I put the phone down, feeling even more deflated following the change of direction my evening just took. I got up the next morning and the sun was shining, so I decided to cut my grass and do a bit of gardening. By 14.00, I was getting peckish so I went home to see if I had a message organising the day and if not, thinking of cooking myself some lunch.

No messages.

I cooked, ate and sent a message asking, "What were the plans for the day?"

No answer.

I tried to ring

No answer.

I rang again two, maybe three hours later.

No answer.

Later that evening I finally got a text message saying, "Will be in touch Sunday."

He came over on the Sunday afternoon on his way to another mate and stayed for a cup of tea. I asked him why he was so insistent not to see me.

He said, "I can't see you when you are unwell, it wouldn't be good."

"I am not sure what you mean. I am actually very well, you can see for yourself."

He agreed with me and started to make plans for an evening in the week; he finished his tea and left.

I had that Monday off and late morning the doorbell rang. It was Inter flora delivering me a massive bouquet of flowers. It put a massive smile on my face. I thought,

"Bless his little cotton socks, he realised he was a bit of an idiot by not being supportive and he regrets it now and is trying to make amends."

I read the card, the flowers were from my work colleagues who I had told about my eye news and wanted to cheer me up.

It's complicated.

The constant gardener

First date, a massive bunch of flowers! Flowers are always a pleasant touch. It makes you feel special and there is nothing wrong with a little chivalry every now and then. Sadly, this didn't happen very often on a first date. Needless to say, I really liked it.

The meal was nice and he was the perfect gentlemen! We had a very pleasant time; there was plenty to talk about and I must have let slip that I liked dark chocolates because on our second date I had a massive box of dark chocolates. How thoughtful!

Each time we met, I had either flowers or chocolates. He liked to cook and often invited me to his house and cooked me really nice food. For our date on Friday the 13th, we had a lovely meal and he gave me thirteen boxes of my favourite chocolates to mark the date. Very nice. And a bunch of white roses.

We dated like that for a few weeks and then I went on holiday with friends. He offered to pick me up at the airport, but we had booked a minibus for the eight of us, so I declined the offer and thanked him.

He offered to go shopping for me and then cook the day of my return which I thought was extremely thoughtful and kind. I accepted. I came back on a Saturday. As promised, he turned up at my doorstep with a bag full of groceries and little goodies.

He cooked. Lovely!

We went to bed and I was very jet lagged and fell asleep straight away.

On the Sunday morning, he woke up first, kissed me gently and whispered, "Do you know what I would really like?"

I thought, "Yes, I think I could guess what you would really like, but lied: "No, I don't know. Please tell me."

"I would really like to cut your grass and sort your garden today."

[*Well, I guessed incorrectly then!*]

I wasn't prepared for that and retorted, "Knock yourself out," and I went back to sleep, thinking it was a little unusual, to say the least. What was he really after? My garden? Do I look that green?

He cooked again and carried on working in my garden for the entire day. Then he said he loved gardening and had many ideas about where to put my flower pots, what type of flowers to get, etc. He said he would love to finish cutting the hedge, the fig tree and mentioned that my shed needed repainting.

He added, "I have a couple of days off this week, do you mind if I come over and finish?" I certainly didn't mind. I don't like gardening at the best of times and was grateful for the offer. With that organised, he left in the evening.

As planned, he returned on his days off and worked his socks off. My garden looked beautiful. I was really pleased. I was still wondering where the catch was. It came soon enough.

He was a carer on a zero-hour contract. I understood he had three or four clients he was looking after in their homes during the days sometimes at night. Then all of a sudden this dried out. He wasn't sure quite why, some story about not being required, being difficult, etc… anyway. I was sure something was going to turn up; there is no shortage of care work I am sure.

At the weekend, out of the blue, he messaged me: "I am in town with my children, can I come over?" I had people round that day and didn't think it was appropriate to meet his children that way, nor was I entirely convinced I needed to meet his children as I was still concerned about his true motives.

Then the following week, he said he had no work. I wasn't quite sure how to respond. He explained that he would not be able to pay his rent and if he was evicted we won't be able to see his children anymore. As he won't have anywhere for them to sleep.

Indeed, that was very sad.

"Do you need any help?" I offered kindly.

"Yes of course," he replied with a beaming smile, "that would be nice."

Eager to be helpful, I invited him to forward his CV

for me to look at it and perhaps assist him in finding alternative employment. I also offered to look for care worker agencies in counties nearby, as well as in London rather than just Sussex, for him to ring. He appeared hard-working – he certainly was as far as my garden was concerned – and experienced. I was convinced he would find something very soon.

The text came back: "All the best."

The scam almost worked.

It's complicated.

Seven Days

If you are not a cynical person, then online dating is the best way for you to become one very quickly and give you serious doubts about men and leave you to ponder about what prompts them to act as they do. Towards the end of my online dating days, I communicated with a new person. Not too much to write home about, but in comparison to previous people I spoke to, he appeared normal. He lived locally and we had things to talk about. He was charismatic and I must confess I was drawn to him.

I thought we had quite a lot in common, similar take on life and aspirations. Once again, the subject of his ex was a little repetitive during our meetings but by that time in my dating experience, I knew what to expect and let it wash over. He had warned me on our first date that there were going to be three people in that relationship, the third person being the mother of his child. I am still not totally convinced it is the ideal topic of conversation for a first date but was becoming immune.

I must admit that constantly texting his ex during our date was a little off-putting. He went on, saying that various girlfriends over the past years had complained about his ex always being in the picture and had proven to be the reason for his previous relationships to fail. I thought it was very good of him to admit where it went wrong in the past but a little daft not to learn from past mistakes and to ignore it and do nothing about it.

Anyway, I was in two minds about seeing him again mainly due to the omnipresence of the ex but thought, "Nothing ventured, nothing gained," and agreed to go on another date. We met up for a pizza and the monologue started with his past. Again, there was little evidence in his conversation suggesting he was looking for a bright and happy future with anyone else but the killer was yet to come. He went on, saying that after he split up with the mother of his wife, he brought home seven women in seven days.

"Why?" I asked, wondering not only why would you want to do that, but more importantly why would you feel the need to tell me? Is this really a good idea?

"To see if I could?"

I can understand that after a split your self-esteem is hurt. Your mind is tortured and you may want to boost your ego by seeing if you still appeal to the opposite sex.

However, seven in seven days is pushing it and certainly doesn't demonstrate too much concern for those women.

"Was the experience as satisfying as if you had stayed with the woman you care for for seven days?" I enquired candidly.

"Of course not. It's always better with someone special," he answered.

"Why do it?" I asked still failing to understand the reasons to do it [am I unique and too old-fashioned here?] and even less the reason for sharing it with me. He didn't answer, probably not wanting to understand my question.

I continued by asking, "What would you call me if I had had seven guys in seven days?"

He looked at me puzzled and asked, "Are you calling me a slag?"

Errrrr, let me think about it…

It's complicated.

Self-centreed or what?

One thing I found out about men when dating online is that they like to talk about themselves. Listen, not so much, but if you lend them an ear, they will go on and enjoy being at the centre of your world. Although only when it suits them. If you try to have conversation / contact on your terms then it is called being needy. And we all know that is not a good trait! Like it or not, this is a very common theme when online dating: men like to talk about themselves. A lot.

Once again, the first contact was established via computerised selection and the picture looked half decent and the profile genuine enough, so we got chatting. We exchanged a few emails, had a few discussions about what he did. In that all-important initial stage, you want to find out more about the stranger so that he stops being a stranger.

The conversation topics were mainly about him. He didn't show any interest in me. Could it be because women are more curious and ask more questions? Or maybe I am just plain nosy and want to find out more about people. Anyway, correspondence was very much one-sided and also extremely sparse, not to mention irregular.

Sometimes there was a three-page *War and Peace* type of message and then nothing for three days, which of course left me in limbo. Is he ever going to offer an answer? Is he playing hard to get? Eventually, the invite for a first date arrived. Lunch or coffee? On the one hand, lunch – even coffee – suggests that there is a time limit, a natural break so to speak, so that you don't need to pretend you have left the dinner in the oven and you need to rush home when the date is not what you were hoping for.

The expected time associated with a lunch hour is usually an hour if it takes place during the week and you are working. We had agreed to meet in a pub not too far from both our place of work. Close enough, so I didn't have to spend my lunchtime driving there and back; then again, not too close, you don't what to face half of the office during that crucial first date!

Luckily, we both knew such a pub and agreed to meet there. What we hadn't agreed upon was whether the food was going to be involved or not. I couldn't decide whether to eat before the date or after, or hope that an offer will be forthcoming. It's not always easy.

In this instance, I boldly assumed that lunch would form part of the date. I arrived with a minute to spare. I knew the area very well, knew where to park and I was there on the dot so as to maximise the hour, should he be good company. I glanced at all singletons in the bar. No one there looking remotely like the guy on the picture. Five minutes passed, nothing. Ten minutes passed, still nothing, where is he coming from? His previous message had said that he was working only fifteen minutes' walk from the pub. So even if he crawled and left at the time of our meeting, he would be arriving shortly.

A little voice in my head seems to wonder. Am I being stood up?

Difficult to say.

I had given my phone number the previous day to say let me know if something crops up and could I have yours too should I have a last-minute emergency and find myself unable to come? That message remained unanswered.

I looked at my phone in case he decided to actually warn me he was late, on his way, etc. By that time, he was over fifteen minutes late and I decided to go back to work. I downed my soda and lime put my coat back on and as I was leaving, he came through the door and greeted me.

"Hello there, nice to meet you at last." *[You very nearly didn't! An apology, possibly, for being late could have been in order. So late and no manners. Good start!]*

He followed his greeting by asking me if I wanted a cup of tea? I come from a coffee-drinking nation, so I had to decline the tea. Something else, possibly? Sadly, no mention of food. I had quite a lot on in the afternoon at work and opted for another soft drink. We found a table and started to talk.

When I say conversation, I mean monologue, because I didn't manage to say much at all, it was all about him, his childhood holidays abroad, his hobbies, old and new, his work and his clients. I am not even sure he paused for breath. On the plus side, no mention of his ex, nor his children for that matter. All very riveting, but the clock was ticking and I could see the point when my work restaurant was about to close and I would be left without having any lunch.

After half an hour of listening, I said that I had to go back to work. "How long do you have for lunch?"

"An hour."

In this instance, I also had to go back to work and allow myself sufficient time to purchase some food before my lunch break was up.

I thought I was extremely diplomatic in not mentioning the fact that:

❦ He was late; and

❦ When you meet someone for lunch, and you said exactly that: "Shall we meet for lunch?", the expectation is that some form of collation will be available. My lunch break was actually being utilised for another purpose and I was getting hungry.

I said my goodbyes, lied that it had been nice to meet him and left.

The following evening, I went back online, thought maybe I had caught him on a bad day and thought I would perhaps send a few lines, only to realise that he had blocked me!

Blocked!

I couldn't believe it!

I was absolutely sure I hadn't said anything rude, controversial or anything that could have displeased him, as I hadn't said anything at all besides cutting the monologue short.

It's complicated.

Would love another date

Once again, I had exchanged a few emails over a period of time with a new gentleman. Some people prefer to meet straight away, which is good in a way as you don't waste too much time in telling your life story again, only to find out that he is not going to be the right guy for you.

Some prefer to drag it on a little and as a result, you correspond for a number of weeks until the first date is actually mentioned, which leaves you wondering at times whether he was only chatting to you and weighing his options before meeting you.

Anyway, the first date eventually arrived. It went smoothly, lots to talk about, a few waves of laughter. Sometimes, the date that starts as a coffee or a drink extends into a meal and you end up spending three or four hours. Time goes quickly and you end up thinking to yourself, "This is going somewhere." And this was one of these dates.

At the time of departure, he asked me if we could meet again. Yes, of course, I was thrilled at the prospect. Time flew by and I really enjoyed the afternoon. We decided to meet again soon.

The date was followed by a few text messages and I was beaming. "So far so good." The expectation of a second date was looming.

Was it really?

Eventually, I understood that it wasn't going to follow despite the eagerness felt at the end of the first date.

It was followed by a strong sense of déjà-vu with the pitiful set of excuses of why a second date couldn't take place: The Sick Grandmother, the VAT return to be done, the unexpected 'rain check' and finally the long and only too eloquent silence.

Or the one and only offer: "Shall we go to Frankie and Benny's at 8.00pm Tuesday?" followed by no further communication if you said you couldn't make Tuesday.

Back to square one.

It's complicated.

6

• • •

VERY LUCKY ESCAPES

First blocked number

I had a serious case of holiday blues. I was just back from a great skiing holiday with other singletons I had never met before on one of my many solo holidays. I had a fantastic time and came back on the 14th of February. Double whammy of gloom for me. Holiday blues coupled with a Valentine's evening alone.

Although, I had vowed I would never go back online and suffer yet more soul-destroying rejections, a friend of mine had told me to register on the dating site she was on. She went on saying that she had two successful dates and was going to see again the second guy again. He seems to be great fun. She told me his name where he was from. She finished by saying it was a very good site and I should go to it.

Peer pressure! I wanted a successful story too and I caved in. As it turned out, it was the site where I encountered all the scammers, in less than a couple of months. To my mind, it was by far the worst site. I naively trusted her judgment and registered on the 15th of February. Within a few hours of putting my profile up, I have a few 'likes', which boosted my sad ego.

One of them started a conversation in the morning of the 16th. I read both the message and profile. Not quite the guy I would go for, but I answered nevertheless. As it turned out he had the same Christian name as the person dating my friend and he lived in the same town. My answer came: "Are you all called John in Essex?" and explained that my friend, and I gave her Christian name – was also on the very same site dating someone with the same name from the same town. Coincidence?

He assured me that he didn't know my friend and he was pretty much a one-woman kind of guy and we carried on messaging via the site for a while. Then we exchanged phone numbers and started to talk via WhatsApp.

Most days, I woke up to a message from him and I also noticed that he had viewed my profile or my pictures almost on a daily basis. He told me he was smitten, he couldn't wait to meet me, etc. We talked about football, the various activities we were into, pretty innocent. It went on for a few weeks. One day, he messaged me that I was the first thing he was thinking of in the morning and he was falling asleep thinking of me.

Naturally, I enjoyed the sentiment. He said that we had to meet, that he couldn't wait to meet me. He added that he was sure I was going to be so worth the wait. I wasn't sure to be able to live up to such expectations but always ready for a challenge.

I said that I couldn't do that weekend and suggested the following weekend. To which he answered he was away on business to another part of the country. That's when the penny dropped as well as my face. My daughter was present when I read the text and she said, "Mum, what's wrong?"

I had met my friend that week who told me things were going fabulously with her new boyfriend. He was so sweet and things were going well. She also told me that the following weekend she was free as he was going away on business and told me where to. It wasn't just the same name same town coincidence, now it was the same business trip to the same place on the exact same weekend!

Oh yes, the charming boyfriend was chatting me up whilst going out with my friend. I decided to tell my friend because if he started chatting me up, he was most probably chatting up other women too. I also told this lovely gentleman that I had understood he was dating my friend, which he first denied then said, "Arghhhh."

It took me ages to find out how to phrase my message to tell her about the guy she thought so lovely. I wrote the message. Read it again, sought my daughter's approval and sent it. She answered, telling me she thought it was entertaining because he had told her that he had cancelled his membership to the site and she knew he wasn't on it. She added that the previous night they had gone to her mum's to be introduced to the family and they stayed over.

Interestingly enough, that was the night I received the message that his last thoughts were for me! What a rat!

He might have stopped paying his subscriptions but clearly, his profile was still on there and he was still pretty active. I stopped contacting him. However, he was still looking at my pictures on my profile on a daily basis and commenting too. I am not exaggerating; every day I had a view, a wink online from him.

I told him not to contact me anymore. Which he did for a couple of days, then I noticed he was still looking at my profile and thought of reporting him, but he hadn't really done anything worth reporting. He was only trying to do what others do as a matter of course.

He contacted me again on WhatsApp, sending me pictures and making plans for when we'd meet, even though there was really little chance of us ever seeing each other. "When your friend introduces me to you," he said, "please wear the dress on your profile to make my life complete," I told the little pest where to go and started to dread that day should it ever come. I told him to get lost time and time again. I also tried the gentle approach: you wouldn't like if my friend was chatting up other guys. Nothing seemed to deter him. I was getting tired of this and asked to be left alone or I would tell my friend he was pursuing me. He did for a day or so.

Meanwhile, I noticed, that my friend had unfriended me on Facebook, which really upset me. A few weeks passed and I found out from the grapevine that she was still seeing that creep and gathered from that that our charming gentleman may have told a few lies about me, which could have been the reason behind the Facebook unfriending.

To this day, I am still perplexed by her logic: why would I have gone out of my way to tell her about her cheating boyfriend if I was really interested in him? It would have been much easier to say nothing at all. I was pretty hurt about it, to tell the truth, really cut up as I thought she was a good friend and I had done nothing wrong. I had done what any good friend would have done: protect her from a two-timing lowlife.

Unfortunately, people judge you from their own standards, or standards of the people close to them. In her case, very close to her, deception and cheat were thriving.

For the sake of future encounters – as we were part of the same group of friends – I chose to forgive the unfriending and also the right go she had one day about me, talking about my behaviour. *[MY behaviour?]* Apparently, I was talking about her behind her back, when my only question was to find out if they were still together, since he had started to contact me again.

I decided to copy his lovely messages where he explained that it would be fun if he could set me up with one of his friends and double date. As if! Where he said I was really the woman for him, etc., thinking that maybe one day I would actually demonstrate who was doing the chasing. She probably still thinks I tried to steal her boyfriend.

Thinking back, with such high morals and values they were a match made in heaven. I did download all the messages he had sent me on the site and the WhatsApp messages and saved them on my PC, thinking that one day I would show her who was actually doing the chasing and what I kept replying to him.

Anyway, the story didn't end there. I received new messages from him and I became determined to try new tactics to shake him off. I started ignoring him. After all, it takes two to tango if he sends a message and I don't answer. Eventually he will get the message.

That made him very angry and he flooded me with messages throughout the day. His last message that day was also extremely revealing, where he revealed that once he had what he wanted from my friend, we'll be free to start our story. I couldn't believe what I was reading. I deleted his number and thought it would be sufficient.

The end came soon enough, as he had predicted. I was flying back from America when I received a message ending with when can we meet? Which made me smile. *Seriously?* I never answered.

When I went back to work the next day, I asked someone to show me how to block a number. I should have started with that.

Unfortunately, blocking his number proved to be futile and he carried on texting me from various mobile numbers.

Now that I knew how to block, it was simple to repeat: Settings – Phone – Block – Enter number.

I was gathering quite a list!

It's complicated.

QPR 1: Me 0

Another guy got in touch with me who was local with a similar age and profession. It looked as if we did have a common ground. For once, the computer algorithm seemed to have been correct.

After a week or so of emailing back and forth at the rhythm of one email a day, I suggested that we could possibly meet in a local pub and perhaps see each other face to face. I thought it would be easier to get to know each other. At that rate of answers, it was going to take us years to determine whether we were suited for each other or not.

We decided to meet in a pub halfway, which turned out to be fairly noisy *[note to self: public place, yes, but crowded noisy pub, possibly not the best!]*. The conversation was not flowing easily, leaving us with long blank spaces and I couldn't get any questions to produce more than monosyllabic answers. It was painful.

Then he mentioned football. I quite like football; I also enjoy rugby and any sport really. I prefer watching sports live, rather than on TV. I thought we were onto something and welcomed the start of new topics of conversation.

His love of football was undeniable and in particular, his unconditional love for a specific Premier League club and we went through a list of recent matches, goals scorers, statistics, poor refereeing decisions against the 'Golden Club' of course, etc.

And then he ended what hadn't even begun with a simple sentence: "I am really looking for a girlfriend outside the football season, the rest of the time I have football and I am quite happy just with football during the season."

It's complicated.

Just making my ex jealous

As I mentioned previously, a vast proportion of men online are still in relationships, some still very hurt because the relationship has ended but they haven't accepted it. Being left for someone else is never pleasant. It's mental torture. I am very well placed to know.

However, it never gives you the right to mess with and hurt someone else. It happened to me. It happened to my friends. Some guys are just dating to make their ex jealous in a desperate attempt to get them back. It is a painful recurring theme. I had started to communicate with a guy, really enjoyed our chats, we met on a few occasions and it went really well.

I liked him and I thought, "Yes!" We definitely could become an item. His wife had moved on with someone else and from his conversations, I realised that it was still pretty raw, which is perfectly understandable. We went on a few dates which I thoroughly enjoyed and I thought the feeling was mutual.

We eventually decided to go on a weekend break together and with the thought that this dating was going to go to another dimension, and I was both nervous and excited at that prospect. At the time, my daughters were still living with me and every other weekend they were with their dad and gave him dates where I would be free. He said that since the mother of his kids had just gone on holiday with her boyfriend for two weeks, it shouldn't be a huge problem for her to look after his children for a weekend. He also added that he was long over due a break with someone. I was happy.

The weekend never materialised, when he did request permission to go away for the weekend, he was told: "If you meet HER again you'll never see your kids again." I never saw him again. It was entertaining in a way that he had to ask permission to go away for a weekend when she had been with someone else for a while and had been on holiday with her lover.

Anyway, using your kids as emotional blackmail is one thing, but going along with it is quite another. When questioned about it he just said: "Well for the sake of my girls I have got to try and patch things up; I do love them and can't become an absent father. I need to stay and try again." Patch things up? Try again? According to him, she had been with another man for over two years.

To me the two statements didn't really match, she had moved on with someone else and from what I gathered she wasn't going to leave him, so that would make an interesting 'ménage à trois'. Was that the patching up?

Well, good luck to them. In my opinion, he had used me to make her jealous and it had worked.

How could you possibly stop the father of your children from seeing them? Especially if you enjoy much time alone with your new lover. Someone needs to look after the little cherubs. What a lot of rubbish. I was really upset; I thought you haven't really sorted yourself out and you started something else and made a fool out of me and hurt me. Sad creature of a man! No wonder she left you!

A few months later, I checked his page on social media. I really couldn't tell what pushed me to do it as he had unfriended me but not blocked me. I supposed it came up as people you know and you may wish to become friends with, in case the unfriending had been done by mistake. In any case, I was able to have a look and he was there happily married to someone else. I concluded that the 'patching things up' didn't quite work and within six-nine months met someone and married her? That was very quick by any standards.

Mind you only a few months prior to that he had also been declaring his undying love for me, clearly not that strong but felt I was better clear of that worm. A couple of years later, he contacted me through Facebook *[scary after a couple of years]* and sent me a message to apologise for his behaviour. He explained that he wasn't in a "good place".

To tell the truth, neither was I, but I didn't go around and hurt people. That's the difference. I accepted his apologies but told him exactly how I felt.

It's complicated.

Variations on the same theme

"When you come around mine tonight, can you make sure you leave your car right in front of my drive so if my ex drives past she can see I have a visitor?"

Scary thought. Your ex has nothing better to do than to clock the cars in front of your drive on an evening?

"Let's put something on Facebook – perhaps that photo of the two of us last week. I know that my ex checks my pages via my son's account." Another woman with nothing better to do. She left you, is now married to another guy and now she is stalking you? Really? Let's stay clear of Facebook.

"If my ex-wife comes to the door during the meal [*mmmmm*] take something off when I go and open the door and come to the door and get me." Trust me, if someone comes to the door, I am not removing any piece of clothing, if that is what you are referring too, nor would I come and get you.

Since we are on the subject, should your ex come at the door and say, "Hello, I made a terrible mistake, maybe we should start again?", what would you do?

[Long pause]

Actually, too long a pause for anyone's comfort. She has already come back to you previously from what you told me and left you each time for another guy. How many chances does she need?

Still hesitant?

Goodbye from me!

The same should apply if at the question: "If your wife came back now, would you go back with her?" He answers, "I don't know." Then you have your answer. It's clearly time for you to move on. He is still pining for her.

I even encountered the all dreadful ex-wife once, actually the very first time I went to his place.

I had been invited for Sunday lunch. I arrived and after the drive to his place, I asked where the toilets were. I went upstairs and as I came back down the stairs, ended up face to face with the woman he had been calling all sort of names, not very polite ones at that, ever since we first met. She was, by his accounts, by far the evilest creature on this earth. I must admit, I was taken aback when I saw him smiling at her and asking her to stay for a cup of tea. *[Was I dreaming the scene?]*

She had the decency to decline the offer. She obviously was curious to see me. I then became the bad guy when I dared ask what she was doing there. I found it very unusual to invite and offer a cup of tea to someone you have described as the lowest form of creature on the planet.

How wrong of me to query that?

It's complicated.

From stingy to spongy

We had a few dates and it was all going reasonably well. Then one day we went out and he asked, "Can you give me some cash to pay for my petrol as I forgot to get some cash out?" At least this one hadn't forgotten his wallet, just forgotten to get cash out. So, I went along with him and put £10 in HIS car then at the checkout he asks the woman at the till: "Could I have twenty Silk Cut with that please?" That was my cue to say, "You can put the Silk Cuts-back, I'm buying your petrol home not feeding your addiction." Which earned me a nasty look, but never mind.

The following week he offered: "I'll cook you a meal this weekend."

"Very nice," I thought. When he arrived, he announced that he hadn't had a chance to go shopping on his way from work, so off we went to the supermarket and got some food. We arrived at the checkout... oh, I forgot my wallet at home. *[Again?]* I certainly could see a pattern emerging here. I paid nevertheless for the lobster, the wine etc. I suggested that the following week we could go out and see a play.

"Are you free Saturday and I'll get the tickets?"

"Yes, very good idea."

I got the tickets and told him there were £25 each. The answer came as: "Oh I am a bit skint at the moment."

[What a shame!] "Not to worry, I can offer the ticket to a friend. I know she wanted to see the play, so she can have your ticket."

I didn't feel that was the anticipated answer.

When we met for our next date I noticed that he was wearing a new suede jacket. I commented on how smart it looked and he said, "Hope so, it cost me £130."

"I thought you were skint!"

It's complicated.

Bobsquarepants: the ultimate sponge

This one was my first encounter with the male gold digger, not that I have that much gold. As hard as it may sound, he did me a massive favour and contributed to me being able to recognise the other spongers later on in my dating life. I had been alone for a while, both daughters had left home for university by now and I felt it was really time to start afresh.

I met a guy and we went on a few dates.

We went out for almost a year; I thought he was sweet and handsome. My daughters thought he was taking advantage of me from the word go but I didn't listen to them and continued dating him regardless.

There were a few differences in our lifestyles and background and I saw that he could appear to be disproportionate but I didn't mind. I studied until I was twenty-seven years old, I have a good job and I have accepted other the years that I may not always have a partner matching my career. He had a low-paid manual job and had many debts inherited from the time of his marriage that he was still paying off. He had been pretty open about them and I said when you can contribute, do. Meanwhile, I sponsored our holidays and lifestyle.

After eight or nine months he moved in. Close to our first anniversary, he proposed! I couldn't believe it! I was over the moon. I thought things were going well for me at last and to tell the truth I didn't mind being the breadwinner and provider of everything. I was happy and, as they say, ignorance is bliss. We went away in the summer and he purchased a ring.

A month or so later, I was making plans to move my daughter to university and he said I am not there that weekend. I enquired about his whereabouts and he had made prior arrangements with his ex-wife's family to help someone move out.

I was livid.

1. I was on my own to move my daughter and could have done with some help;
2. Making your own plans is one thing. Perhaps check with your fiancée / wife-to-be, first to make sure it doesn't clash with anything else; and
3. Why on earth are you going back to the past if you are still paying the debt incurred there? Why are you still helping? I couldn't comprehend his motives.

I also noticed that we actually had not seen his daughter with me since he had proposed. He had ensured he saw her when I wasn't present, which I didn't mind as she was the most obnoxious, rude and lying young woman I have ever had the misfortune to meet.

I had bought her a Christmas present – quite a pricey one – and I did not even get a thank you. When she was coming around my house for tea, she couldn't bring herself to say hello when she was coming home to eat the food that I had prepared for her. Never a 'thank you', 'it was nice', nor a 'goodbye'.

However, all of a sudden he always chose to see

her away from my house which was out of character. Something wasn't quite right. I was wondering whether he had actually told her he had proposed. One evening, I decided to get to the bottom of it and said, "Tomorrow, I am going to the registry office to book a dates" which was followed by a massive silence and a very very long face. To tell the truth, it wasn't the reaction I was expecting.

Eventually, he said, "So you know then."

"Know what?" I knew something wasn't quite right, I didn't have a clue what it was and certainly wasn't expecting what was to come.

"I am still married."

"And when were you going to tell me?"

"I was going to divorce, but I couldn't remember my wife's date of birth and I would have had to ask my daughter for her mum's birthday and I really couldn't do that."

"No? Why?" I had heard some poor excuses in my life, but that one had to be the worst.

"I don't want her to know we are divorcing."

Twelve years after his wife left him for another guy and left him to pay the many debts, he still could not get around to telling his twenty-one years old daughter he was divorcing. Pity that didn't stop him from proposing to me! Not the best evening of my life!

At least that explained why she hadn't come around; it would have been a bit awkward to see a ring on my finger. I am still wondering today how long he would have been able to carry on the pretense. The next day he came back with the form from the court to start the divorce proceedings. He did ring his daughter, in the end, to find out his wife's date of birth.

He completed the paperwork for the divorce which brought the most amusing story: he had a tattoo on his forearm with the name of his wife and their wedding date, which he had covered prior to moving in with me. On the divorce paper, you need to give the wedding date. As it turned out, the divorce form was sent back, the application for divorce was rejected as his wedding date he had tattooed on his arm was incorrect!

That was priceless! At least this entire fiasco gave me a reason to laugh.

He restarted the divorce application, this time with the correct date. Second time lucky! I asked if there was anything else he had kept away from me. I was hurt but still felt sorry for him. He assured me that there wasn't, he wanted to spend the rest of his life with me and not her. I wanted to forgive him for deceiving me, but he was on thin ice.

The final blow came a couple of weeks later. He had asked me to search his paperwork to look at something for his car and I found his latest bank statement. It worried me and gave rise to a new difficult conversation. It transpired that since moving in with me, he had changed jobs for one with fewer responsibilities and therefore with much less income.

He obviously no longer needed to pay rent nor bills as he was living with me so only required income to pay his debts and sponsoring his kids and stepkids. Being a leech was clearly his lifetime ambition.

Why carrying on working hard when you have found a mug to support you?

It's complicated.

Desperate

This happened to a friend of mine who had been dating online for a while just like me and we met once and she told me the most incredible story. Like me, she had become extremely cynical about the entire online dating affair, but still had time running on her subscription so she cancelled the next payment and instead of asking the site to delete your profile, she removed all her pictures and the majority of the information on her profile and forgot all about it. Until one day – I can't recall why – she went back online and saw a message, which she thought was worthy of an answer they corresponded a little and decided to meet for a meal.

They arrived by the restaurant, she recognised him, of course, and introduced herself since he didn't know what she looked like. Without a word of hesitation, he declared, "I have booked the table for 20.00 and the hotel from 21.30."

Going back to my Polish film, the main character arrives at her date, the guy is already in the bar, stands up and greets her by the wrong name and says, "My place or yours?"

To which she answers, "Are we not staying here for a drink?"

Sad and disappointed face from the guy: "Ah, you want to talk first."

Although this particular situation never happened to me, speaking to some of my friends, it is actually not an uncommon situation at all.

Once again, not sure whether to be pleased or offended by it.

It's complicated.

Scammers

Naturally, being online for such a long time, I was sure to encounter the famous 'scammers', which happened on one particular website. The funny thing is, it was textbook security guidelines. Both were caught by my smile and both in the army posted abroad and made the first contact.

Exactly as the website had warned.

Both received the same answer from me: "Thanks for your email, but I am not after a long distance relationship."

Scammer One messaged me telling me about his wife dying and him needing to recreate a sense of normality. Although not in so many words, nor in the usual poor grammar but in a weird kind of way.

I was half-torn to say leave me alone and half-tempted to see if he was for real. So, answered a few messages, he was doing most of the talking and probing.

Was I living on my own? [Yes, most of the time.]

Was I lonely? [At time, yes.]

Wouldn't it be nice to find someone and go for walk

by the seafront? *[Possibly if in a warm country, in English grey, wet and windy weather, not too much.]*

He wanted that very much and he felt he would like that with me. *[Flattery may not lead you anywhere.]* He went on saying it would be much nicer if I downloaded some form of instant messenger so it would be better to chat. He enjoyed our chats very much and missed me when I was at work. *[Don't you work too?]* Yes of course but weird hours.

Then he sent me a picture of him a seven- or eight-year-old boy and another couple. *[Who are these people?]* Me, my son, my sister and brother. Do you have pictures of your family? *[Yes – many but none I am going to share with you.]* A couple of days went without messages. So much for the instant messaging application. He explained that were his sister and brother in law who was looking after his son while he was abroad, it was better for him to be there. *[Without a doubt much better than a war zone.]* His sister and brother in law lived in America and his son was there. *[America?]* It was tough for him, he missed his son and his wife… but now was time to start a new life with me; he was ready.

I asked what sort of music he listened to when he was posted abroad. It took two days for a response to arrive. "Diana Ross and Michael Jackson."

"Nothing too recent then!"

One day later.

"What about you? What type of music?"

"At the moment listening to John Legend."

"Yes, I know him, I would love to chat with you and hear your voice, I already love you so much."

"After a week's worth of messages?"

"Yes, don't you?"

"No, this is going nowhere, I don't want a long-distance relationship and someone who is likely to be abroad half the time."

"I am to come to the UK soon, then we can meet."

"Tell me why you would come to the UK if your family and son are in America?"

"It would be better if we could talk."

Two days passed.

"Yes, I am going to be able to come to England it has been agreed with my boss, I miss you so much."

"Miss me? You have never met me. Besides, you'll have to leave again, so maybe you should meet someone who wants a long distance relationship."

"I think we need to talk on the phone."

Another day passed. Meanwhile, Scammer Two had replied to me: "No, it wouldn't be a long-distance relationship, I don't want that either."

"Do humour me and tell me how this is going to work?" I never had an answer.

I received on instant messenger a new message from Scammer One: "I am looking forward to talking to you so much."

"Are you?"

"Yes, the only thing is I need to buy a phone card."

"Phone card? Where on the planet are you? Here on earth, we use mobile phones!"

"I am far away, I just need some money to buy a card

to make an international phone call." *[Do you now?]* The software was immediately uninstalled from my machine all messages deleted.

I went online to the dating website straight away to report him as a scammer. I searched the site for a phone number, a link something to report Scammer One. Literally at the same time an email pops up in my site inbox, email along the lines of: "We noticed that you have been in communication with Scammer One and Scammer Two, their profiles have been deleted from the site as we found out the content of their messages and profiles to be inappropriate."

Someone beat me to it, literally by a few minutes.

It's complicated.

Not with a barge pole

I had been messaging this guy and to tell the truth, it was one of the few where I can't even remember his name or where he was living, but I clearly remember the circumstances. The first few conversations didn't ring any of the usual alarm bells and we agreed to go on a date. He suggested a restaurant in a town halfway between us. I agreed.

I got ready, texted just before leaving to ensure he was still planning to make that trip – always worth checking that you are not going to be stood up – and went. We met, not looking too much like the picture but I know that many people do not take a good photograph.

We sat down and whilst looking at the menu he confessed, "I am in between jobs at the moment and I am not sure I can afford a meal." *[Well, perhaps you should have suggested going for coffee rather than a meal, but you know what they say, there's no such thing as a free lunch.]*

I answered: "Let's just go Dutch and just have a main course and no alcohol." With that agreed, we started making small talk and starting to get to know each other. We started discussing hobbies and we had one in common and with this, we had something to talk about. He said that for a few years he was in such a group but had a disagreement with a guy and then had to leave, joined another group, but the wife of a guy actually misunderstood him and created rows and bad feelings within the group so he had to move on to the group he was currently in.

I am in a choir, an orchestra and in a drama group; rarely have I witnessed those kind of arguments or fall outs and in drama, there are a few egos to consider. People have different views, different personalities and at times have a moan and a grunt but I have never seen anyone leave any groups because of it. Hobbies are there as a distraction from day to day life and we are all there to enjoy the same activity. I thought that was a bit extreme, and the same thing happening twice?

Anyway, the main course and beverages got ordered and the conversation went on: "How long have you been 'in between' jobs?" I enquired.

"Quite a while in fact, there had been a disagreement at work *[I can see a pattern emerging here].* It was all a misunderstanding. I was working in a school and allegations were made against me *[don't like the sound of that – you don't leave your job without another one for a misunderstanding]* which I didn't like and left, thought I would not have a problem finding another job and in fact it has proven quite difficult."

"I know I am risk averse, so the thought of leaving a full-time job without having another one is very risky in this day and age."

"I thought that with my experience I would fall into a job."

[Quite self-confident with it! There is a small line between self-confidence and arrogance, please don't cross it!]

"Competition is tough these days *[and potential lack of reference may not help either]*, so how do you manage financially? Did you win the lottery?"

"Lol, no such luck no. I am still living with my girlfriend *[not another one!]*, and when we bought the house together four or five years ago, I put all my savings in the purchase of the house but now the situation is difficult as we no longer get on, so I am looking for a job and a new place to live until the house is sold and I get my share, but it is going to take a long time because I put most of the capital in the house."

"Are you not seeking to see whether she could buy your share out, then you could move on, at least move out?"

"…"

"That's what I would do," I concluded.

"Yes, maybe but it's difficult to talk at the moment; we argue all the time." *[I wonder why. You are the boyfriend who keeps on giving.]*

Dinner arrived, we eat and the discussion turned to food, décor, service etc… keep it safe, and this is when you think to yourself: I can't wait for this meal to end, ask for the bill and leave as far away as possible.

Not my type at so many levels!

Finally, the meal ended, the bill was split and settled. We went back to our respective cars. Before we parted, he commented on how well we got on, which I must say did surprise me.

Everyone I know tells me on how my body language and facial expressions always depict my thoughts and feelings – which, trust me, is a curse. They were all missed here. We parted. I was breathing a sigh of relief and I went home.

Usually, after a date where I was taken out, I thank my date. Being polite doesn't cost anything. In this case, there was no need for that and left it at that. A couple of days later. I receive a message asking me how I was when we could meet again. He had such a lovely time and he thought we got on 'like house on fire'.

Naturally, I wanted to let him know that this was not going to go any further and another date was not on the cards. I thought I would speak to him rather than send a text message. So I decided to ring his mobile phone in response to his text. I thought that in this situation a voice call was preferable.

I rang and it was cut off before being answered. I presumed he was busy, which was odd as I had just received the message. Left it a little while and rang again. The same thing happened. So, I left it, thinking I would clarify the situation a little later.

An hour or so later, I got another message telling me: "I couldn't pick up my phone as my girlfriend was in the room with me and I couldn't talk, I'll ring you when she goes out tonight."

Another one of those who was the only one in the relationship to believe they were separated. Not wanting to wait for the coast to be clear. I texted back: "Please don't contact me again."

A very simple sentence, I thought, which he had a problem understanding and which prompted a stream of text messages, a dozen or so phone calls. All appearing as missed calls, until the moment I decided that enough was enough and blocked his number.

It's complicated.

On the same theme

There are a few sentences that I have heard on a first date that made sure it would remain just that, a first date. "I am still employing a private investigator to know the whereabouts of my ex-wife."

"How long has it been since she left?"

"Seven years. She left without a forwarding address; I needed to know where she went. It took me years but I have managed to track her."

[A little extreme. Possibly psychotic? Maybe there was a good reason why she didn't want to be found? Let's keep it to the one date, shall we?]

"I have been separated from my wife for fifteen years and we are still in court to agree on a settlement." From my point of view, it takes two to tango, where I can agree that one partner in the relationship may have a shorter fuse than the other, but there is also the option to let go and give in for a quiet life, especially after fifteen years!

If I understood correctly, the new relationship will be punctuated with attendances to court. If you haven't moved on after fifteen years, are you ever going to?

Unfortunately, the going to court with the ex – even when there were no children involved – is a bit of a common theme. I didn't enjoy splitting up and sharing the assets with my husband, nor with my long-term partner, but it never lasted that long. There is a problem if that isn't resolved after so many years.

"My wife tried to kill me." *[I don't want to be in the way next time she turns up… just to be on the safe side. Goodbye.]*

"There a restraining order on my ex-girlfriend." I had two or three restraining orders on ex-partners.

It's complicated.

Jeremy Kyle material

I must have been very naïve, but for years I thought guests on the Jeremy Kyle show were actors. I thought very good actors providing an excellent entertainment.

There was a point in my life when I started studying for additional professional examinations which coincided with my daughters GCSE and A level exams and we ended up revising at the same time. One of our guilty pleasures was to reward ourselves after a huge revision session by watching a sneaky episode of *The Jeremy Kyle Show*.

They laughed at me when I confessed that I thought the people on the show were actors. My daughters tried to convince me they were not acting.

I only found out they were right when I encountered a couple of men who could have been on the show during my dating years.

Extract of conversations:

"I have been married three times. The first wife left me soon after my daughter was born. One day I came back from work she had left and I didn't know where she went. So, I went to the pub." *[As you do when you are heartbroken, drown your sorrows.]* "And the barmaid was very understanding, we started chatting and one thing led to another and three weeks later she fell pregnant."

[Bit quick, isn't it?] I like the 'falling' pregnant.

[Let's wait for it, my money is the baby was a bit premature, she saw you coming mate.]

"She was pregnant and we moved in together it wasn't easy because but a few months later my second daughter was born – a beautiful girl. I would give my life for her."

"Naturally," I said. "All dads have a little soft spot for their little girls."

I had to ask. "Was she born prematurely?"

"Yes, how do you know? Yes, about six weeks. She was so strong that they left her to leave with her mum straight away."

[Did they now? I must be psychic!]

"Then we lived together and a couple of years later we got married. It wasn't easy because she already had two children of her own from a previous relationship and she was bartending and I had now to support three kids while trying to get access to my eldest." *[It goes without saying.]*

"Now I have ten step-grandchildren. My stepdaughter was pregnant before she left school, but she didn't stay long with the dad, he was into drugs and he is now doing a twenty-year stretch at Her Majesty's Service."

Then he went on how the numerous step-grandchildren came about and I struggled to follow how many different partners, who was what where and when. I gave up before the third wife story and made my excuses.

THAT was complicated, and yet he had failed to say so!

Another story, another tête-à-tête which went like this:

"I have two daughters"

"So, have I!" So far, so good, I thought.

"The youngest is getting married shortly."

"Congratulations."

"She hasn't met the groom for very long, neither her mum nor me knew she was seeing him."

"Is she usually a private person?"

"No, she is not private at all. I think the marriage is a scam to get money."

"What makes you say that?" I enquired naïvely. In my experience, parents are quite happy for their children to get married, proud even, even when they disapprove of the bride or the groom. I had never known anyone to admit it could be a scam.

"I just think it is. She needs the money for a lawyer at the moment, she is facing criminal actions against her, she was arrested recently and going to court. Since she has just recently come out of jail for dealing drugs, she hasn't been able to find a job and needs money to get a decent lawyer to defend herself for the next drug dealing offense."

"I see."

"She is a nice girl, you'll see, I mentioned that we were going on a date and she is keen to meet you."

Not as keen as I am NOT to meet her. I quite like my life free from drugs and criminal cases and intend to keep it that way, thanks.

It's complicated.

AA material

Alcohol has also been the cause of some embarrassing and unpleasant moments of my recent past. There was a recent question on a TV quiz show asking whether people on a date would prefer a fussy eater or someone who drinks too much. The fussy eater would win hands down!

I had agreed to go to the cinema with one of my dates. Having finally come to an agreement about the film – by basically letting him choose what he wanted to see – we went to the cinema the following Wednesday evening.

We had purchased a few sweets to munch along and I noticed that, like me, he had brought a small bottle of water with him. Although mine was in my handbag and mine was water. His was in his pocket and wasn't water. As I found out later, ignorance is indeed bliss. The film started and so did the drinking and as the film progressed he was getting louder and louder in his comments, making me feel uncomfortable, irritated and embarrassed.

He clearly exasperated the other people around us, who were giving me unfriendly looks and were asking him to be quiet. I didn't know where to put myself. I eventually told him to button it and asked what was wrong with him. He proudly stated that to make the cinema experience even more enjoyable he had filled the bottle of water with vodka. Of course! What else could it have been?

Considering he had chosen the film and that he was going with his date, you could have been tempted to think that the experience was already suitably enjoyable enough without having to resort to alcohol. At times, I am wrong and I must recognise it!

To tell the truth, the cinema incident was the second and final blow. The previous weekend had already been a painful experience, also due to an over-consumption of alcohol. We were due to go and meet some of his friends on the Saturday evening. He said that we would stay at home during the day as he wanted to catch up on some paperwork; he asked if I could help him with some of his finance stuff and I agreed, thinking the quicker we finish the quicker we can go out.

At lunchtime, he went out to the local off-licensce to buy some beer and vodka for the party later. He left me at home with the paperwork. At the time I didn't think anything of it.

He arrived home and opened a beer and we continued on the paperwork. I noticed a few more beers were opened and he saw me looking and he asked if I wanted one. I don't like beer so the answer was no.

Early evening, we grabbed a takeaway. The beers were gone and he opened the bottle of vodka. The paperwork hadn't actually progressed much but we cracked on. When I lifted my head, the bottle of vodka was half-empty.

"Are we not going out this evening?"

My car was in the garage and I couldn't drive and by that point neither could he.

"We are, what's your problem?"

"You have drunk well over the legal limit."

"I am not drunk, any copper stopping me I'd show that alcohol doesn't affect me."

"I am not going out with you and will not let you drive!"

I continued on his paperwork still and he finished the vodka – neat – and announced, "That's enough for today, let's go."

I experienced a little déjà-vu with the next part of the conversation.

"We are not going anywhere," I insisted.

"I am not drunk and could show you," he declared loudly, starting to slur his words. He went on attempting to demonstrate that he was still able to walk heel to toe in a straight line. It goes without saying he was far beyond that point and as the straight line he was walking in was incredibly wavy.

"Let's stay here this evening and we can join your friends for the BBQ tomorrow."

The original plan was to spend the evening there, stay over and then have BBQ on the Sunday. He got extremely angry and said that I was changing my mind all the time [???], he had enough of women like me [it has happened before, maybe?]. No one could tell him what to do. He was going to show them and he was going to the party with or without me.

"Where are my keys?" he enquired.

"Where you left them," I answered with that little white lie as I had half-guessed his next step when he was so keen to show me how sober he was and I had moved them just slightly out of reach, not by more than a few centimetres, but I knew it would require potentially clearer thoughts and better coordination to get them.

He searched in vain, got even angrier and shouted we were over, OVER, OVER. No one told him what to do and not even me. No one. This was the end. He had enough of me. We were finished.

I was taken aback, but I also realised that he was under the influence so didn't react. Still unable to find his keys, he went to the spare bedroom and I didn't hear a peep from him all night.

The next morning, I heard the front door and his car leaving. He hadn't uttered a word to me and I was upset as I thought he would have calmed down. Besides, I hadn't done anything wrong besides doing his paperwork when he was drinking.

I came downstairs and saw that he had left his unfinished paperwork on the kitchen table. This time I certainly wasn't going to do anything with it. It was a pretty uneventful Sunday. The evening came and went. Just before 21.30, the doorbell rang. I went to open the door. It was him. He had a bunch of flowers, he said he hesitated to come over as he remembered we had words.

[WE *didn't have words, YOU did.*]

He couldn't remember what he had said and he was sorry.

[*That's what happened when you 'are not drunk' you have difficulties remembering what you did.*]

I filled him in with the previous night's conversations, he apologised again, he didn't know what had happened, or what had come over him. *[Alcohol, perhaps? Who could tell?]* He didn't want it to end and he was never going to do that again.

As it turned out, not until the following Wednesday.

It's complicated.

One Easter, I was coming back from a fabulous cruise with my friends and despite the brilliant time we had, I couldn't help thinking that it would have been even better if I had shared these times with a significant other. Once again, my holiday blues got the better of me and I registered onto a website, a new one, where I felt things would be different.

As per usual, the first couple of weeks boosted my ego. New members always get a lot of attention and I must say that particular first message caught my eye.

In May, we decided to meet and our first date was at a local food and drink festival. I liked my food and, as I found out later, he liked his drinks. We had a truly enjoyable day and decided to meet again, and again.

It was going well. In early July, he invited me over for Saturday lunch. "Come over, we can have lunch. My sons will be home and you can meet them, in the evening we can meet my friends and then go home on the Sunday morning."

That's sounded like a good plan. I offered to make and bring dessert, suggested chocolate mousses, thinking the boys would like them. The offer was gladly accepted. What could have gone wrong?

I arrived Saturday as expected and dinner was ready with a bottle of bubbly in the fridge. The meal was really nice and I had a couple of glasses of bubbly. I remember telling him that I rarely drunk at lunchtime. I generally drink a little and I am a real lightweight. His sons didn't join us at the table. They came down to pick their plates of food and then later on to pick a couple of the chocolate mousses I had brought. We briefly greeted, happy to meet you etc, but really that conversation didn't last more than a few seconds. I had met teenagers before and nothing was out of the ordinary with that meeting and behaviour. They went straight back to their bedrooms.

After the meal, he offered to go for a stroll in town and show me around town. I thought it was a great idea and I followed. It was a very sunny day and we left the house. We soon arrived at a pub, where he said, "Shall we have a quick one for the road?"

He was on first name terms with the landlord.

He had a couple of drinks to my spritzer and we carried on our walk and ended up on the seafront. It was a truly glorious day and we sat in the beer garden of yet another pub. I thought it was time for me to have a soft drink as I felt I was already out of my comfort zone. Then another pub where we stopped for a while and we just chatted.

The afternoon turned into evening and he suggested, "Shall we go for something to eat?"

"Yes, I am feeling rather peckish," and we went to a nearby restaurant. We ordered food and drinks. I thought I'd only have a glass of wine with my food and

I should be fine. My glass never emptied and by the end of the meal I was very happy and without a care in the world! As arranged earlier, we ended up in the pub with all his friends and once again was offered a drink and I remember ordering spritzer with a huge amount of soda and a glass of water.

I also remember standing up from the bar stool I was sitting on to go to the loo and saying, "No, I can no longer walk," and sat right back on the stool. Everyone laughed and I didn't touch my drink there and drunk water. I didn't feel bad and carried on talking to everyone, although the landlady admitted to me a few weeks later that I was actually very funny that night. Still unsure today how to take that.

Anyway, closing time came, we ordered a taxi and went back to his place. I must confess that I don't remember the ride back. I remember thinking it was strange that he knew all the names of all the pub landlords. As I walked up the stairs I felt unwell, not well at all. I was so over my limits and the rest of the night demonstrated just how much over.

As much as you wish to remain elegant and glamorous when you are in the early stage of a date, the consequences of drinking too much tend to achieve the exact opposite. Possibly not the most attractive start to our sharing a night together!

I should have known better! Then again, I promised myself to never let myself stoop so low again. I finally managed to fall asleep in the early hours of the morning. The daylight was peering through the curtains and he was fast asleep. I thought, at least my throwing up hadn't kept him awake and was thankful for that very small mercy.

By 9.00ish we woke up. He offered me some breakfast. I couldn't face it. I had a couple of cups of coffee and went home a couple of hours later. Apparently, he had never seen such a lightweight. Then again, I had warned him. Lesson learned for me, I was going to pay much more attention to my glasses of wines during our meals together.

The following week, he was organising a BBQ on the Sunday with his friends and suggested that his mum and dad may be coming over to meet me. He suggested that I should stay over after the BBQ on Sunday night and make my way to work straight from his place on the Monday morning. It sounded good, although I thought it was a bit too soon to be introduced to parents. He assured me that he had talked to them about me and they wanted to meet me.

I took being introduced to the parents as a sign of being genuine. Surely being introduced to Mum was a good sign. He reassured me that he had never uttered a word about the events of the previous week. All his mates knew and that was bad enough! It is one thing making a fool of yourself, quite another when there are many witnesses unlikely to forget! Despite my original fears, I accepted. I arrived on Sunday morning and had brought my work clothes for the following day.

We went shopping for the BBQ. Judging from the amount of food and drink he had bought I thought that many people were invited. We went back to his place and started the charcoal going.

The BBQ went well; it was a lovely sunny English summer day. We had been lucky with the weather. Only a few of his friends turned up and I thought we have certainly gone wild with the food and drinks. His mum and dad were very nice and it wasn't at all awkward. They were full of praise for dessert, another one of my specials that I brought over. Alcohol was flowing but I was very cautious not to repeat the previous weekend's experience and kept to soft drinks. By mid-afternoon, everyone was merry, it was very jovial and it was turning into a truly enjoyable afternoon. I noticed that all the beers had gone, most of the wine too.

I thought, good job I stayed clear of the alcohol or I would have been remembered for all the wrong reasons again. Early evening, his mum and dad called a taxi and went home, leaving the two of us enjoying the last rays of sunshine in the back garden. A new bottle of wine was opened and this time I accepted a glass while munching on the leftovers and continuing chatting. The bottle of wine was empty before I had a chance to finish my glass and the bottle of white rum purchased that morning was taken to the garden.

As the evening was closing in, it got a little chilly and we went indoors. By which time the bottle of rum was empty too. Luckily, another bottle of wine was found, I thought it was remarkable that there was still one to be opened. I had another glass. Our conversation moved on to Facebook. I cannot remember how or why but it did. As he was starting to slur his words, I offered to call it a night and go to bed. The offer was rejected, the night was young and the drinking went on. I remember thinking that I wouldn't like to get his headache the next morning.

He suggested that we should become friends on Facebook. I couldn't see any obvious reasons to say no and I agreed to it. He invited me, I accepted. Then he started to go through each and every friend on his account. Who they were, how he met them and giving me a little resume for each one of them. The first one or two profiles I thought were OK but was starting to despair when I realised that he wasn't just giving the highlights, nor picking on perhaps his best friends, relatives, etc. Everyone on that list of friends was being introduced to me. Alphabetically! I was rather hoping the list wasn't in the hundreds of names.

We were methodically going down the list and I feared it was going to be a LONG evening! With the added slurring of the words, it was becoming challenging. It went on until one profile was displayed and everything stopped. No talking, no explanation. Nothing. Silence.

It intrigued me and I was desperately trying to have a peek at the picture and see who that was. Clearly, something happened when he saw the picture. I couldn't see anything and was hoping he would move on to the next one. After all, I hadn't prompted anything. Neither the going on Facebook never requested information on his friends and family.

He didn't move on. He snapped and got so very angry. "Yes, it is an ex-girlfriend, and so what? You can't imagine a fifty-year-old without a past."

[I wasn't.]

"What's wrong with you?" he added.

[With me?]

"We went out for a few months and it ended. Not for me." He was shouting at me by that time.

I didn't understand the sudden change of mood. If it wasn't for you then it is all good that it is over? Of course, I made sure to remain absolutely still and made no comments as I certainly didn't want to cause any more anger. He was clearly agitated. His eyes and his voice were a clear indication that now wasn't the time for any sort of answer, not even a light-hearted one. There is a time for jokes and I quickly realised that wasn't one of them.

He carried on ranting, stood up and got right in my face, pointed his finger at me and shouted, "And this is why you and I will never work." *[You don't say. Still, I would like to know what I had done or said but I am not brave enough to ask.]* I was genuinely regretting my two glasses of wine. Big mistake!

I was trapped with a screaming guy, angry at me for something – I wasn't even sure what – and I couldn't even drive home anymore. He went out for a cigarette and I took the opportunity to unfriend my new-found friend, gather all my things and go quietly upstairs.

He followed me soon after, I was as quiet as I could be, not wanting to awake Mr Hyde again. He put his head on the pillow and went straight to sleep and I breathed a sigh of relief. I finally fell asleep and we were both woken up the next morning by the alarm clock. He went downstairs and I had the quickest shower of my entire life; a cup of coffee was waiting for me when I came down and he smiled as if nothing had happened and declared, "What a good day yesterday, we must do that again."

I nodded although my immediate thought was: "Not if I can help it." I said I was running late and left as quickly as I could to ensure that I was ahead of him in the traffic. Considering how much he had drunk the previous day I wasn't convinced he was OK to drive.

It's complicated.

Real stalker

Another likely consequence of online dating is having the misfortune to meet a stalker. At first, everything seemed normal, he was nice and considerate and we went for a few dates. I explained very early on that whilst I thought he was a very nice guy, there was no chance of us becoming an 'item'. The chemistry just wasn't there at all, besides which he lived a fair few miles away – 100 miles exactly door to door which was also a suitable deterrent for a relationship! I told him that I enjoyed his company and would like for us to remain friends. He assured me it was absolutely fine. We continued seeing each other and as the weeks passed, I introduced him to my friends as another friend; went to parties and quizzes. It was all pretty civilised at first and then it started.

He had given me a voucher for a pamper which I thought was really sweet, so I had said to him, "I am using your voucher tomorrow, it has been a tough week at work and I'll be seriously enjoying the indulgence."

"Excellent, I hope you have a good time."

"I shall, I am booked in for the afternoon."

The next day arrived; I received a little text: "Hope you have a good day."

I thought, "Bless, he remembered I am going for my pamper," and I answered, "Actually, on my way now, really looking forward to the pamper, thank you very much it was truly a nice gesture."

I parked the car, went in, put on the robe and the slippers, put my phone away and noticed two or three messages from him, but thought that I would answer after my treatments. And off I went. Perfect bliss for a couple of hours. Then, I went back to the changing room, changed back to my normal clothes and noticed many texts and missed calls. I thought something had happened and immediately rang back.

Nothing had happened, he just wanted to know where I was. I replied that he knew where I was and suggested he should re-read yesterday's messages.

I had not only told him what I was doing on the phone, but I had also messaged him. I was at the spa day he kindly gave me.

"You were not answering my calls."

"No, I didn't have my phone in the treatment room."

I thought that was slightly odd but didn't think much of it and carried on seeing him.

The following days, there were many text messages, again asking me what I what I was up to, where I was, etc. and thought he was just trying to make conversation.

I went to his place a weekend soon after that and met his friends and we all went out for dinner. During the meal, the conversation came to Valentine's Day and proposals, etc., and he turned to me and whispered, "If you asked I would say yes, you know," and I laughed it off.

I said: "You are a very good friend, but I have no intention of marrying anyone at the moment." The evening lingered, later he added out of the blue: "One day you'll change your mind."

"Maybe, but don't hold your breath."

A few weekends later, we decided to go to an evening out with my friends and he stayed at mine. Obviously in the spare bedroom, it never entered my mind that he could be sharing my room. That wasn't on the cards, I have male friends, and that is exactly what they are – friends, no benefits, no possible confusion. At 8.00am a knock on my bedroom door, at 8.00am on a Sunday after a late night, I wasn't exactly impressed.

"Shall I make you a cup of coffee?"

"Yes, it would be lovely in a couple of hours!"

The rest of the Sunday was becoming very awkward, especially at lunchtime when he gave me a piece of jewellery. When I saw the box, I wasn't sure how to take it. I could recognise the Tiffany box and thought, "Wow, I love Tiffany," but then thought it was a bit much, a bit expensive for friends. As it turned out it was inappropriate.

I usually like Tiffany jewellery and that particular one I didn't like – it was a ring to make matters much worse. I couldn't accept. I just couldn't on so many levels.

The day finally came to an end; my daughter was due to come back from her weekend away and I was keen to spend time with her. I was also keen for my friend to go home and not overstay his welcome. Not considering whether I had already made plans for the evening, he asked, "Maybe I can stay over this evening and go straight to work tomorrow morning? I have brought my work clothes with me."

"I don't think this is a terribly good idea, as I have made plans with my daughter."

After a good half hour of debates as to why he couldn't stay, why he wanted to meet my daughters, he eventually went home.

On the Monday morning, I was getting ready to go to work and the phone rings, it was him. I was running late so I didn't answer. Then the text messages kept on coming, one after the other. The phone rang again and again. Well, I heard it vibrating, because my phone is always on silent.

I finished my race to get to work on time. I had a 9.00am meeting which I was in serious danger of being late for. So, I drove, parked, straight to the meeting room. Phew! I had made it!

When I returned to my desk I had about six or seven missed calls on my mobile phone, three voicemails on my work phone, messages, emails on my work email address and two on my home email address. I texted back quickly to tell him to calm down, that I was at work and advised him that I was not being paid to answer his phone calls, that I'll ring back at lunchtime. I did so and asked what and the urgency was: he had a good weekend and he missed me. One text message would have perfectly sufficed and I was starting to believe there was something seriously wrong with him.

And the texts asking what I was up to continued to flood in.

That week I had planned to go out for a pizza with a couple of friends from choir. During the day, like every day, I had a message from him wishing me a good day. I always thanked him and wished him the same. That day he also enquired if I had any plans for that evening. I told him I was going for a pizza with friends I hadn't seen in a while and was looking forward to it. After work, I had a message: "What are you going tonight?"

"Same plan as this morning, going for a pizza."

"What time?

"7.30."

"Where?"

"Is this the Spanish Inquisition? In a pizzeria!"

I was starting to get a little uncomfortable with the level of curiosity in my evening. I went for my pizza. One of my friends had problems with her car and didn't arrive till 8.15pm, we sat down and ordered at roughly 8.30 – 8.45. By 9.00, my phone started vibrating. I ignored it as I knew who the calls were from. It continued vibrating. I finally picked up and I heard his voice saying, "Where are you?"

"I have already told you."

"It's gone 9.00 now and you are not at home."

"Yes, I know. I am still at the restaurant."

9.30pm, the phone rang again; I picked it up and he announced, "You are still not at home, I am outside your house and there are no lights!"

"You have driven 100 miles to tell me what I already knew?" I asked in disbelief.

"You should be home by now!"

"Please don't ring again, I am having a nice evening with my friends and will be home when I feel it is time to go home and it is going to be much much later, so please go home."

"I want to see you and I am outside your house."

Was he really waiting for me outside my home? A little extreme, possibly freaky too.

"Please go home, you are not seeing me tonight, I am with my friends and when I come home it'll be late."

I went home feeling terribly nervous that he would still be there, but there was no car, no sign of him. I went to bed and it took me ages to fall asleep. Next morning, I got up and for once I sent the first text: "Please don't contact me again."

At lunchtime, I went to B&Q to purchase an additional lock and a chain to put on my door. I was a little concerned about his behaviour. I wasn't quite sure how to put the lock on, but the B&Q assistant was brilliant. I went home and put the locks on that evening. Still undeterred, I kept on receiving messages asking me where I was, what I was up to and the even emailed me asking me what WE were doing at the weekend. We are not doing anything at the weekend anymore, mate. You had a chance, you blew it.

It's complicated.

Not over your ex

I was online one weekend searching for local emerging talent and saw that someone from the next town was actually contemplating my profile. He winked; I suggested that rather than him reading, perhaps we should meet up in a local pub and actually meet rather than message. He agreed and we met a few hours later. He didn't really look much like his profile picture but as I understood later, he had been on site for a number of years.

We had a drink and chatted. Chatted may be a slight exaggeration because he had nothing to say besides his job and football. Sadly, none of which ignited a passion within me. I tried to get him on music, films, etc., not successfully. I asked pretty basic questions too, to try and spark an interest that we would have in common, but the answers I got were a vague yes, or no, and I felt he really didn't want to be there. As a result, time moved ever so slowly. When he finally finished his drink, he asked me if I wanted another. I was compelled to decline. I was under the impression that I was going to meet someone new to have a conversation and try to establish some sort of rapport or connection, and there was no sign of this here. It was more like a wasted journey and I went home.

The next morning, I received a message from that guy, telling me he thought we shouldn't meet again as I wasn't over my ex. I was intrigued to see how he could have possibly reached that conclusion as, unlike him, I hadn't mentioned my last long-term relationship. As it happened, it was well over five years previous and as so much water had run under that particular bridge, I rarely mentioned it.

I felt I had to ask him what gave him that impression. Obviously that was totally irrelevant as I certainly wasn't fishing for another date, but felt I needed to know what had prompted him to say that. Most probably nothing. It was his way to tell me he didn't want to see me again. I messaged him saying that if he didn't want to see me again that was absolutely fine by me, but why have to invent an excuse? Why not come up with 'we have nothing in common, let's not meet again'? Way closer to the truth. Besides, he hadn't actually wowed me with his sparkling personality!

The answer came a couple of days later: "Indeed, I have been very quick to judge." *[I was being judged!]*

"Perhaps we should go for a meal and give you a second chance."

The sad thing is, I did agree to go for that meal when I hadn't even enjoyed my first chance.

The day of the meal arrived a few days later. The food was awful, one of the worst meal in my entire years of dating and the company was just as dire the second time around, only it lasted longer!

You live and you learn.

It's complicated.

7
. . .

THE END

All good things must come to an end; in my experience the best thing was the end.

I agonised over the ways to end whatever had started. 'Relationship' is too big a word to describe what was really happening. Meeting your date again to tell him seemed like a waste of time and effort. More often than not, they were still seeing other people so you would be wasting not only your time but theirs. They may not even wish to hear from you again anyway.

Phone call? Text? All seem a little cowardly.

Generally, you have had a date, maybe two, and they leave you, always saying it would be nice to meet again. Of course, more often than not, as my personal experience demonstrated, what they mean is in another life because half the time they have no intention of seeing you again anytime soon.

I always thanked my date for the evening, flowers, etc. as the case may be, which prompted a very quick message followed by absolutely nothing. Eight times out of ten there are no messages forthcoming so you think well no point in pursuing it. Let's move on to someone a little more interested.

Here some of my best messages received:

- 🌱 *"See how it goes."* Sitting on the fence after telling me face to face what a lovely evening it was and how much we had in common. I thought that was an odd thing to say and as a result didn't hold my breath for another date. Indeed, I never heard from him again.
- 🌱 *"yu are not ovr yr ex."* Which I actually translated as 'I am not over my ex' because the only date we had was a monologue about his break up.
- 🌱 *"I have started dating someone else."* Oh, as well as dating me? That gives an entirely new meaning to double dating.
- 🌱 *"You are very nice but I have decided to go back to my wife."* I understand. You couldn't cheat on her with me so you thought you would try elsewhere? Good luck to you.
- 🌱 *"I have decided not to date."* Meaning decided not to date ME anymore because your profile is still very much online and you have just uploaded new photos.
- 🌱 *"You remind me of my wife."* Not the best compliment since you spent the past few months slagging her off and from all accounts, she didn't have the best record at being faithful to her three previous husbands. At least, I was faithful to my only one. Not the kind of woman I like to be compared to!

In the majority of cases, you saw them one day and then there was complete silence the next. They were happily texting you a few times daily until the date. You met and then nothing. It all came to a halt.

I still really don't see what would have been so difficult in saying, "I do not think we are compatible, there was no spark there, let's agree not to pursue it, good luck in your search," or something to that effect rather than the poor excuse I was given.

Clearly that was far too much to ask!

In most cases what I got, if not a pathetic message, was complete silence. Hard to comprehend when the date had been pleasant. Which left me wondering: had I said anything that could have been offending? And I ended up going through the entire date in my head again. I couldn't help wondering what had gone wrong and fell into the trap of messaging once, thinking that maybe he was as unsure as I was and someone needed to make the first contact after the date.

Sadly this rarely led to an answer. It's the cue to give up and move on. Silence or no silence, there is only so much rejection a girl can take. There is no point wondering why and what is wrong with you. If he couldn't be bothered to tell you he wasn't interested, then clearly, he was not right for you.

It's complicated.

You WILL dump me!

There are so many experiences of the silent treatment a girl can take!

I had been on a few dates with someone, everything seemed to be going well. So I thought. There were regular messages, the occasional phone calls and we had been on a few dates. All of a sudden and for no apparent reasons my messages remained unanswered. I understood he was a busy man; he had a job, many responsibilities, travelled a lot and I took the lack of response as a sign of being busy. Nothing had led me to believe otherwise.

After a couple of days, I enquired to know how he was. To tell the truth I was expecting a 'it's manic at work at the moment' or something to that effect. But nothing was forthcoming. I didn't want to sound desperate or clingy so I thought there was no point in insisting. I got the message loud and clear; he had decided I wasn't for him. Fair enough. But he was going to tell me exactly that.

All busy executive that he was, he was going to act like a man for a change!! And I decided to force the issue. To be honest, the last date had been, once again, close to his work and he had been late, again, and I was the one who had to travel.

The conversation had been dreary about his meetings that day, his work problems and his son losing his credit card and how he had to contact his ex-wife to sort it out and that wasn't going to be a pleasant discussion because they were not on speaking terms, etc.

Nothing breathtakingly interesting. Not wanting to sound heartless, I also had meetings during the day and managed to make my way on time to the date, and quite honestly, potential arguments with his ex were no concern of mine. I would much rather discuss other things on a date. Besides, when you lose your credit cards the best thing to do is ring your bank. Not your ex-partner.

Following that last and possibly dullest evening, I wasn't particularly bothered to see him again. I had always made the effort to go and see him, he was busy and talked of very little else than his work. He hadn't really made any effort to get to know me so thought unless we did something else at our next date. The option of going to a restaurant for an hour right by his work to hear about his problems had already lost its appeal.

He may have sensed it which may have been the cause of his silence.

Maybe I wasn't suitably worried or sympathetic about his son losing his wallet. I couldn't tell. However, I was perfectly aware of what was happening and I was getting the 'I'll stop messaging and she'll soon get the gist' routine.

But I thought, no. You know what, you are a big boss, in both senses of the word, man up and tell me you don't want to see me again. Quite honestly, the feeling was extremely mutual, after three meetings I had been bored out. Another one whose wife had probably died of boredom somewhere along the line. I thought, "I am not letting him get away with just stopping messaging me and moving on." I wanted it spelled out.

I sent a message: "Would I be correct in thinking that you have decided not to see me anymore?"

He took the bait and broke his silence immediately with a very, very, long answer, when a simple yes would have sufficed. A real gem of rubbish about me finding the right man for me who would make me happy (well, to tell the truth, I would have settled for just a little less dull than him), and it went on and on. Without thinking, I deleted the wasteful prose, but with hindsight should have kept it for the purpose of this book.

Still, the only entertaining fact about this story is that he had emailed me after eight emails: "Glad you think of me in terms of the next phase of your life." Trust me, I wasn't I was merely trying to plan a date at the time. But it made me chuckle.

It's complicated.

It's not me. It's definitely you!

I saw someone for two, maybe three, months and came to the conclusion that we were not compatible. I didn't think it was working and thought it would be best for the two of us to go our separate ways. I had offered to go and tell him face to face and asked on a Sunday afternoon: "Can I come over?"

"No," had been his reply and I thought I would better give him a ring. I rang and told him what I had to say. I would have preferred saying it face to face but he had saved me a trip, after all, and was grateful.

He continued the conversation by saying I was a very difficult woman to understand and I was sending mixed messages. I thought I was as clear as possible. "I don't think it is working, we are not compatible, it would be best not to see each other anymore," was not a cryptic subliminal message.

A few days later, I was passing his flat with one of my friends, we had agreed to go for a pizza. As it happened, the pizza place was close to where he lived and I thought I would see if he was in and take that opportunity to get the pair of sunglasses I had forgotten at his place.

I rang and asked if he was in and if I could come in and get my glasses back. As I was picking my glasses he said, "I am not sure what you want."

"My stuff back," I replied, irritated.

I had realised he hadn't understood our previous discussion. I thought that actions would speak louder than the words we had over the phone on Sunday. He let me in, I picked up what I wanted to collect, clearly stating, again, it was over and wishing him luck with his new search and left his flat.

It must have been still extremely confusing for him because he rang back a few times over the next few weeks, shouting abuse down the phone. Always the quickest way to a lady's heart and sure to get her to reconsider. No?

It's complicated.

Very silly me

At first, I had thought that one was different and realised after a couple of months that he wasn't. Once again, I had to tell him, in the nicest possible way, that I didn't want to continue seeing him. I saw him, told him and with that, I naïvely thought we had broken up.

He had borrowed one of my jumpers once and we agreed on a time and day for me to go there and collect it.

When I got there, I collected my jumper and I asked for my keys back. Not that I made a habit of giving my keys to anyone, but on this occasion, he had worked near my place one day and we were going out that evening and rather than him waiting for me outside my front door after work, I had said, "Here are my spare keys, make yourself at home, I won't be long."

I just hadn't asked for them back on that day. As a result, a couple of weeks later, when I thought it was time for us to go our separate ways, I asked for my keys that he still had.

He simply responded, "No."

I hadn't planned for that answer! Why on earth did he want to keep my keys when there were no reasons for him to come and see me? He went on by saying that he felt there was something there and he didn't want to call it a day just yet as he thought we could make it work.

Interesting thought. I thought we both needed to be willing parts in order to have a relationship? No? It takes two to tango, as they say, and I was no longer prepared to dance.

Anyway, irrespective of him wanting to end it or not I did. I certainly didn't want to start an argument about it nor going to re-consider my position either, so I went back home as quickly as I could and changed the locks.

You only make that mistake once. Trust me!

Two, possibly three, weeks later, my evening TV viewing was disturbed by the doorbell. I came out and it was him. He had come to see me and came to return my keys and explained: "Don't be too upset, but I feel this is the end of the road for us, you are a really nice lady, but I feel it's not going to work etc."

He was finishing with me, three weeks and a change of locks after I had done it myself!

It's complicated.

My garage is not your personal storage facility

I had the good sense to end it before too long and realised that my garage was full of his belongings. Bits for his car, motorbike equipment – you name it, it was left in there. He had only come over a handful of times! And so, the saga of getting his rubbish out of my garage commenced.

"Can you come and pick them up please?"

"OK, will come tomorrow after work."

I waited, then at 22.00 I messaged, "I presume you are not coming anymore."

No answer.

After a couple of days, I asked again: "When do you think you can pick up your stuff from my garage?"

Still no answer.

I rang and the phone went dead.

After a couple of weeks, I ended up saying, "If coming to mine after work is proving to be difficult, I'll bring it to your best mates' work, on my way to work if that is easier for you."

Of course, that wasn't easier at all, I was being childish and of course, we were all adults. We agreed on another day, I stayed in for the exact same result. I was losing the little patience I had left.

Finally, my next message read, "Will leave your stuff out Thursday evening, you can pick it up then, otherwise the bin men will on the Friday morning."

Remarkably enough, he was there that evening.

How to end it?

In the end, what's good for the goose is good for the gander and I decided to embrace the dumping by text messages too. I remember the first guy that I ended the potential new relationship with by text. It was actually more difficult than I thought. I felt really bad actually because he was trying to be nice guy, bar the tendency to make me feel as if I wasn't good enough for him. Not what I like in a man.

There was not much chemistry anyway so I did end it and said exactly why. He started debating that he didn't know why I was leaving him, he couldn't understand, he was such a nice guy. *[Please read my text again; I have just explained why!]*

With or without a clear ending to the dates, I always deleted all phone numbers. There is no point in overloading my phone memory. Some I blocked because they had been too weird, or offensive or just plain nasty.

It's complicated.

More? Do you want more?

Four of my old unsuccessful dates ended up contacting me years later. They had originally given me the silent treatment hoping that I would get the message, which I did and literally years later, out of the blue, popped up with a little message. Why?

One I had blocked managed to contact me years later on another number. Scary!

Another one contacted me after a while and asked if we could stay in touch. I wasn't sure what would be the point and what sort of conversation we may have, but on the other hand, did not have any argument to justify a reason not to. He had been nice enough on the few occasions we met, sadly not boyfriend material, but pleasant enough. At the time, I had said that I couldn't see any future developing from our meetings and left it at that.

A few months later, he contacted me again, asking if we could keep in touch. I caved in and went for a drink. Not much to say; we chatted about our jobs and children but there was still absolutely no spark and I didn't think there was much point in seeing each other again. He continued the messaging for a few weeks; I responded politely, ensuring that I wasn't encouraging anything or another encounter and was hoping he would eventually give up without me having to resort to the silent treatment I was familiar with.

When he asked if we could meet again, I made some excuse by saying I was busy but offered to meet him with other friends a couple of weeks later. There's always comfort in numbers and he would clearly see that a one to one was no longer an option.

I said I was going for a drink maybe and possibly a boogie afterwards if he wanted to join us. His answer came: he didn't need a matchmaker and the only way he would do anything with a friend of mine was is if it was all of us. Was I dreaming or was he suggesting a threesome? I wasn't dreaming. He had been such a gentleman so far. I had changed my mind, I no longer wanted to even consider a drink and a boogie. I immediately said goodbye and deleted his number.

It's complicated.

And one time it did hurt

During all my years online, the end of a relationship, or whatever these were, always put you back to square one and re-enforced your insecurity. You can't help wondering 'what is wrong with me?'

Generally, even after some deep and genuine soul-searching, the answer remains nothing. You quickly move on to the next one to bring you hope, telling yourself that you will find your soulmate soon enough and meanwhile to carry on enjoying the rest of your life. Despite the inevitable sadness, you try to remain pragmatic about it.

With the dating game, there is always the danger of getting hurt. There is the time that is going to punch you in the stomach so much so that you don't feel you'll never going to stand up straight again. It happened to me. Naturally, after years of dating, I was bound to find a guy with whom I finally felt a strong connection with. With my luck, it was bound to be only one-sided.

In the beginning, we met for a few drinks and a meal. He had such a gorgeous smile. We spent hours on the phone and saw each other as often as possible. The first few months were absolutely fabulous. He even started to make plans for the future, which I had stopped hoping for.

I felt genuinely happy when he was around. We chatted about many topics, he was thoughtful, offered me help with DIY, brought me flowers, but above all had the nicest smile on the planet. I just loved being with him. I thought after all these years of searching for my soulmate, I had found him.

We went to France for a little break that summer. It felt as if everything was falling into place. This was exactly what I wanted to experience with my online dating and hadn't succeeded. He was a perfect gentleman, always nice, complimented me, my cooking, bought me flowers and the occasional little gift. I was smitten. In the early weeks of the summer, we saw each other almost every day. He even told me he was thinking of moving closer to me. Since he was travelling to see me on a daily basis, it made a lot of sense. I was happy and I thought it was going to last. Well, at least little longer than it did.

I felt everything had fallen into place and people around me had noticed too. I looked happier. Past experiences had taught me to remain on the cautious side of prudent when announcing my new-found happiness, but I was considering introducing him to my friends and family.

Then for no apparent reason, he stopped coming over. He always had an excuse not to do so. At first, I understood that he had other things to do. We had spent a lot of time together and I knew he probably had friends to see and just the usual things to do.

Then when he finally came over, he drank very heavily and started being nasty towards me and I really couldn't understand why it had changed all out of the blue. He was such a different person. Everyone can have a bad day and he had been so pleasant until then. I didn't say anything then and thought I would wait till the next time we met to tackle the issue. There was obviously something bothering him.

The next day, I left for work. I had a seriously busy day at the mothership and was back to back with meetings till 15.00pm. By 12.00pm, I noticed I had WhatsApp messages, emails, texts, on my way to the toilets I quickly answered back saying I was busy and and I would call when I was finished. I went and delivered my presentation in the afternoon when a member of staff came in to interrupt to tell me that my phone was ringing and there could be an emergency with my daughters. Being interrupted during a presentation is never a good thing, but when you are the person making the presentation, it is even worse. I rushed to my desk to find I had 18 missed calls! 18! No wonder people came to get me. How embarrassing!

Fortunately, none of the missed calls were from my daughters. They are adults but not exempt from any emergencies, accidents etc. They were all from him. I quickly rang back, thinking he may have had an emergency to justify the eighteen missed calls.

I rang. No answer. I texted, still no answer. I went back to finish my presentation. When it ended I had to rush to a meeting, following which I found a free meeting room at work to ring him back and found out what had happened earlier. This time he answered the phone and I got a string of abuse back. Great!

I rang him again at the end of the day. He didn't answer, and I left it at that as I thought he may be busy, although I was considering ringing eighteen times just to get a page out of his book. But I had made plans for the evening and went out.

I rang the next day to find out what had happened. Since he had never seen the inside of an office, he had problems accepting that I could be back to back with meetings all day. He shouted he KNEW I was ignoring him, he also knew I was lying about being busy and there's always a few minutes to text him.

Which I had done; I hadn't even had a lunch break that day. I took a screenshot of my work diary which I forwarded, highlighting that there was no lunch break in my day yesterday. He admitted that he hadn't gone to work the previous day and had been drinking in a pub with friends and he thought I was just blanking him on purpose.

Why on earth would I do that? Beyond my comprehension. If anything, he had been the one slowing things down. It gave me a smooth transition to the next topic of conversation.

Not going to work is one thing, spending the day drinking quite another!

I asked him directly if that sort of behaviour was a one-off. I had already obtained that particular AA T-shirt the previous summer and was not prepared for a repeat performance. I ended my part of the speech by saying, "Let's pause for a second and see what had happened and reboot and carry on as we were."

That must have seriously irritated him as he said, "I'll save you some thinking time. We are over."

I just couldn't believe it! Completely astounded. Speechless. Not to mention gutted.

Generally, you always see the end coming. You know things are not quite right, you have argued, witnessed an unpleasant behaviour, something. Here it was nothing at all, well, nothing I could put my finger on. It went from everyday the world was good to I only see you occasionally and will ring you eighteen times at the most inconvenient time and dump you in no time at all.

He had taken such a big place in my life after only just a few months. It was a massive shock. I went from happy to misery that day from a simple phone call.

My close friends said that he was punching above his weight and maybe he was, but he also made me contented. I feel they were just trying to make me feel better. It didn't, really. I had let my guard down and was paying the price.

It's complicated.

8
• • •

NO MORE

There is an old French saying that it is better to be alone than to be badly accompanied. I certainly could see the sense in that. I was the living proof of that saying.

In the end, you realise that you have lowered your standards so low, swallowed your pride so many times, sometimes your principles too. You have re-arranged your timetable, made compromises, in the hope of finding a less than adequate partner. Through these years I didn't even meet a guy decent enough to be Mr Average and it hadn't done my self-confidence any favours either! And I ended up being hurt in that process too.

I remember talking to my daughters about one of my last dates. We had seen each other for a few weeks and I described him to my girls as being the best of a bad bunch. They were shocked at that description. They were correct, of course, and I realised that it was time for me to quit.

I decided that enough was enough. I deserved better than all that. I came to my sense and thought of all this time wasted: hours of messages, phone calls, going to and from dates, the actual dates. All a huge waste of time. Besides which, it was also a soul-destroying experience and made me even more cynical than I was before.

So, one November I decided to give up, once and for all. I had enough and wasn't going to put myself through this anymore. I knew that being on my own would actually be a far better option than being with any of them. Not only had I made sure I had stopped any subscription renewals – some carry on automatically – but I also removed all pictures that may still be online. To my dismay, I also found out that this wasn't sufficient. On some websites, my profile was still there to be seen. I had to write to every single site and demanded them to take my information down. Which they did.

Unfortunately, this didn't stop them from sending me regular emails to join for free or offering me to find my perfect match. By then I knew how unlikely that was!

Looking back there was not one that I think was a decent option. I was deluded to think that they would make a decent companion, one I would be proud to spend the rest of my life with. In my short experience, two thirds of them were still married, all but one had lied at some point.

Throughout these soul-destroying years, the rocks in my life were my friends. Always there, attentive and giving me the best distractions, consoling me when the tears were getting too bad, encouraging me and trying to find kind words, supporting me.

I thought you know what? I should make sure I spend the rest of my life amongst them. Concentrate my energy on quality time with the people that really matter in my life.

And I did.

I spent a lot more time with my friends and in particular a friend of a friend who I had known for years. Although we were not particularly close within our group of friends, we were going to the same outings, plays, parties, etc. I knew his wife had left him for someone else and he was pretty down. He was still coming out with the group but after their split, he was not the life and soul of every party. Understandably so.

I first suggested to him the single holidays I had enjoyed so much over the years. I believed it would be a good cure for his misery. It had worked for me. A week with people in the same boat as you, enjoying similar activities and having a laugh would stop you moping. Eventually, he went and thanked me profusely as he had a fantastic time. I was happy for him.

As time went on, I saw more and more of him at our usual gatherings. He was on his own and so was I; as a result, we often ended up as a pair at meals or parties, which I didn't mind at all.

One summer, we had gone to see a play and I offered to give him a lift home. On the way back, he realised that he had locked himself out. He suggested meeting his daughter to get her keys to allow him to go home. He thought he knew where she was and we started a little pub crawl of our own to try and find her. A fair few pubs later, I offered for him to come to my place and either stay in the spare room until the morning when his daughter would have been home and able to open the door for him or message his daughter to come and pick him up from mine on her return from the pub. He chose the latter.

And so started the second part of our evening in my lounge. The conversation was flowing, we talked about everything and nothing, no awkward silences; it felt as if we had known each other for years and years.

He told me about his divorce; the decree nisi had come through. I asked him if she came back whether he would start again and he said, "No chance!" The correct and only answer possible in my book. Whoever was going to date him in the future was one lucky lady. Finally, one man with the decency to terminate one thing before starting another. I was suitably impressed.

The evening ended up in the early hours of the following morning when his daughter finally arrived after club closure and a kebab snack. Despite the late hour, I was pleased to see that he was picking himself up and getting ready for the next chapter of his life. I thought he was such a sweetie.

A couple of months later, I had organised a birthday meal with all my friends and we ended up sitting next to each other and chatting. He asked me if I wouldn't mind joining him for a few activities. I jumped at the chance. I sincerely enjoyed his company and with my evenings free from online dating messaging, I welcomed the chance to go out. We started rock and roll dancing. It was great fun despite my two left feet; we shared a meal on a few occasions and went for the occasional drink. It was wonderful. We chatted and laughed, had a good time.

We didn't have any hobbies in common, as such, but we discovered that we enjoyed similar activities and above all, we loved each other's company. I thought (and still do) that he was seriously good-looking, tall, charming, kind and considerate but never shared these thoughts with anyone at the time.

When we went out he was always looking out for me, making sure the taxi would take me home first, he opened the doors for me. He was a real support when I was lonely on business trips. I remember going to Asia for a few weeks for work and we spoke every day. A real comfort when you are miles and miles away and totally isolated and homesick. He showed affection, care and concern.

He still does.

We laughed at the same things, we were having a genuinely good time. I was happy. I knew his past, he knew mine. I didn't have to recap on anything. Once as he was taking me home from a night out, I remember thinking that I would be devastated when he met someone.

I was dreading losing the little time we had together. He was such a gentleman. I thought, "Your girlfriend is going to be one lucky lady." There was a handsome, genuine, caring man out there after all. We had been dancing that night and he had been generous with the drinks and, thought that I want this not to stop for a very long time.

It did for a while.

As we were going out another Friday evening, we bumped into common friends and stayed for a while and it felt as if we were an item. It is really difficult to explain but at the time I felt we were a couple. Our friends and children saw us so often together that it was an easy step to make.

Of course, we were not an item, and I didn't want to imagine a time where he would meet someone. I was secretly falling for him, not wanting to say anything and risk to lose what we had.

After a few drinks with our friends, we continued the evening with a bit of a boogie at a nearby club. As we were dancing he came over to me and whispered, "I don't want to be friends anymore, I think I want more!" As it turned out my feelings for him were reciprocated.

The cherry on top of the icing on top of the cake!

And it all happened the old-fashioned way.

I was nervous, excited for weeks. The butterflies in the stomach of your youth had returned unharmed. I was happy, beaming and contented.

The search was over.

He is everything I ever wished for and so much more. I haven't looked back since. My future is looking better than ever and it is going to be shared with someone I feel proud to be with.

Surviving difficult relationships and having many false starts has hopefully given me the tools and the desire to build a happy one at last.

After all, it was not that complicated!